OFFICE OF THE VICE PRESIDENT
FOR STUDENT AFFAIRS
CALIFORNIA STATE UNIVERSITY, CHICO
CHICO, CALIFORNIA 95929-0125

EFFECTIVE
LEADERSHIP
in
STUDENT
SERVICES

EFFECTIVE LEADERSHIP in STUDENT SERVICES

Voices from the Field

LINDA M. CLEMENT
SCOTT T. RICKARD

Jossey-Bass Publishers · San Francisco

For sales outside the United States, contact Maxwell Macmillan International Publishing Group, 866 Third Avenue, New York, New York 10022.

Manufactured in the United States of America

 The paper used in this book is acid-free and meets the State of California requirements for recycled paper (50 percent recycled waste, including 10 percent postconsumer waste), which are the strictest guidelines for recycled paper currently in use in the United States.

10% POST CONSUMER WASTE

Library of Congress Cataloging-in-Publication Data

Clement, Linda M., date.
   Effective leadership in student services : voices from the field / Linda M. Clement, Scott T. Rickard. — 1st ed.
      p.   cm. — (The Jossey-Bass higher and adult education series)
   Includes bibliographical references and index.
   ISBN 1-55542-479-1 (alk. paper)
   1. Counseling in higher education—United States. 2. Leadership.
3. Crisis management—United States. I. Rickard, Scott T.
II. Title. III. Series.
LB2343.C55   1992
378.1'94—dc20   92-18758
                                                  CIP

FIRST EDITION
HB Printing   10 9 8 7 6 5 4 3 2 1   *Code 9278*

THE JOSSEY-BASS
HIGHER AND ADULT EDUCATION SERIES

Consulting Editor
Student Services

Ursula Delworth
University of Iowa

CONTENTS

PREFACE

This book is about exemplary leadership in the administration of student services in colleges and universities. It focuses on 210 practitioners in student services who were nominated by their peers as effective leaders; 183 of these leaders are quoted in the book. The study provides a collection of voices, perspectives, and ideas on a wide range of day-to-day and philosophical issues faced by practitioners throughout student services. Because the essence of the study is the voices of leaders, the book is a mentoring tool—a way for leaders to reach beyond their immediate circles. Since the leaders' average length of experience in higher education is more than twenty years, *Effective Leadership in Student Services* represents the best practices of almost four thousand years of experience. The thoughts expressed are uplifting and inspirational, and their publication here is designed to take us beyond the realities of current practice, to a vision of the best that is possible.

This is a qualitative study, which focuses on the themes that emerge as exemplary leaders think about the practice of their profession. The study does not attempt to profile the leaders interviewed, nor does it rely on counting the number of respondents who articulated particular perspectives. It does strive, however, to capture the themes that emerge, how these themes are related, and how they enlarge our understanding of exemplary practice.

Our study draws on the research literature in business and industry, on the literature about college presidents, and on the literature of the student affairs profession. Inherent in this work is the assumption that the literature on leadership can provide helpful insights for practitioners in the field. An equally important assumption is that there are characteristics and requirements of the profession that make leadership in student affairs unique.

Audience

The primary audiences for this book are practitioners in student services, including chief student affairs officers and directors of the functional areas represented by respondents (admissions, career development and placement, cooperative education, commuter affairs, counseling, financial aid, international student services, judicial affairs, learning centers, minority affairs, orientation, police and public safety, registration, residential life, student health, student activities, and student unions). New or entry-level professionals can also gain understanding of the art of effective leadership and draw from the work insights and perspectives that will help them in their positions and careers. Graduate students and graduate faculty in student personnel programs should also find the book a welcome counterpoint to theory, in that the book provides a practice-to-theory approach.

The terminology used here varies. For example, the terms *student personnel, student affairs,* and *student services* appear, as do both the terms *black* and *African American.* The variations reflect institutional, regional, and individual differences among study participants. We have not attempted to impose uniformity.

Overview of the Contents

Effective Leadership in Student Services is organized into three parts and eleven chapters, followed by a resource section. The first chapter sets the context and highlights the background of effective practice: our heritage. Chapter One also establishes the need for leadership in student affairs and outlines the nature of the qualitative research methodology underlying the study.

Part One, which follows Chapter One, focuses on attributes, skills, and institutional conditions conducive to the emergence of good leadership in student services. Chapter Two discusses three constellations of personal qualities that effective leaders feel have contributed most to their success. Chapter Three identifies a collaborative style as essential both to leading and to following and discusses the qualities and strategies that characterize leading and following. In Chapter Four, leaders name the institutional characteristics that have contributed heavily to their success.

Part Two also contains three chapters, which focus on relationships with students, faculty members, and staff members. In Chapter Five, effective leaders discuss the qualities and behaviors that have contributed to their success in working with students. Chapter Six focuses on the importance of understanding the central role of faculty members and on how to realize the potential for positive relationships with them. In Chapter Seven, leaders acknowledge the role of staff members in the success of the enterprise and focus on how good relationships with them are developed and enhanced.

Part Three contains four chapters dealing with the hurdles—whether ordinary or extraordinary—that student affairs administrators face. In Chapter Eight, leaders discuss how they work to minimize crises, and they talk about their crisis-management roles. Chapter Nine covers day-to-day issues involving favoritism, confidentiality, time management, and budgets. In Chapter Ten, leaders discuss a wide range of issues, including identity, gender- and race-related problems, and campus politics. In Chapter Eleven, we conclude *Effective Leadership in Student Services* by discussing how exemplary leaders represent and perpetuate an ethic of care in the student personnel profession and in the institutions that they serve. This ethic motivates and sustains leaders and gives special meaning to their work. Resources A, B, C, and D follow the last chapter and provide information on nominators, nominees, the research questions, and the nominees' backgrounds.

Our book, along with the study on which it is based, seeks to capture the best thinking of effective leaders in student services. Leaders surveyed for the study acknowledge their own imperfections and limitations and recognize that their current thinking is sometimes the product of valuable lessons learned through failure. We want to acknowledge the participants in this study for the leadership that they have provided to the profession, but in so doing we do not wish to glorify them and make them seem superhuman; we understand the danger of "air brushing" imperfections away in the effort to epitomize effective practice.

Acknowledgments

We thank the participants for their willingness to take risks and give of themselves to their colleagues. It has been a privilege to reflect on and work with their thoughts.

Gale Erlandson, senior acquiring editor for the Jossey-Bass Higher and Adult Education Series, who saw the potential of this project, and Ursula Delworth, consulting editor for the series, who encouraged and supported us, deserve our appreciation and gratitude. We also thank Reba Haynes, Janice O'Neill, and Susan Turner for their technical support, organizational skills, and engaging good humor throughout this project.

Linda M. Clement wishes to acknowledge her colleagues in student and academic affairs at the University of Maryland, College Park, for their encouragement and their example. She also acknowledges her husband, Peter, her daughter, Kristen, and her parents, Annamae and Jim Donovan, who over the years have never faltered in their understanding and support.

Scott T. Rickard wishes to thank his colleagues in the Office of the Dean of Arts and Sciences at the University of Maryland, Baltimore County, for their patience and good humor during the three years of the study. He also appreciates the loving support of his wife, Marilyn, his children, Katherine and Scott, Jr., and his mother, Katherine Kirk.

August 1992   Linda M. Clement
                                                 Kensington, Maryland

                                                 Scott T. Rickard
                                                 Bloomington, Indiana

THE AUTHORS

Linda M. Clement is director of undergraduate admissions at the University of Maryland, College Park. She previously served as director of orientation (1976–1982) and as assistant director of residence life (1974–1976). She received her B.A. degree (1971) in English education from the State University of New York, Oswego, her M.A. degree (1973) in college student personnel administration from Michigan State University, and her Ph.D. degree (1981), also in college student personnel administration, from the University of Maryland, College Park, where she is also an affiliate faculty member teaching master's and doctoral courses. She has written book chapters on financial management and values, as well as articles for the *Journal of Liberal Education,* the *Journal of College Admissions,* and the *Journal of College Student Development.* She has served on numerous College Board committees and has chaired the Middle States Regional College Board Council. She has also assumed leadership positions in the American College Personnel Association, including those of program chair of the national convention in 1984 and national membership chair from 1985 to 1988. She is a recipient of the Bernard P. Ireland award for effective work in college admissions.

Scott T. Rickard is executive director of the Association of College Unions-International. He served before that as associate dean in the Office of the Dean of Arts and Sciences at the University of Maryland, Baltimore County (1987–1992), and as first vice-chancellor for student affairs (1980–1987). He was assistant vice-chancellor for student affairs at the Univer-

sity of California, Davis (1971–1980), chief student affairs officer at the State University of New York, Stony Brook
(1968–1971), and dean of men at Willamette University
(1966–1968). He received his B.S. degree (1960) in science education from Oregon State University and both his M.S. degree
(1962) in college student personnel administration and his
Ed.D. degree (1966) in higher education administration from
Indiana University. He is the author of numerous journal
articles, book chapters, and research reports on a wide range
of topics, including career advancement, equity issues for
women and minorities, planning, budgeting, staffing, leadership, and the profession. He was chair of the American College Personnel Association's 1984 convention in Baltimore
and editor of the media and editorial boards (1985–1988). His
service with the National Association of Student Personnel
Administrators (NASPA) includes work on the *NASPA Journal*
(1980–1983), the executive committee of Northern California
Region VI (1978–1980), Region II Advisory Board (1981–82
and 1985–86), and the Washington Office Advisory Group
(1983–1985).

CHAPTER ONE

Leadership in
Student Services

Leadership was once described as one of the most observed and least understood phenomena on earth, with over 130 definitions reported in one study (Burns, 1978). Less than a decade later, more than 350 definitions of leadership were reported (Bennis and Nanus, 1985). Because of the complexities and the highly subjective nature of leadership, it is not surprising that there are a variety of different perspectives on it.

The majority of studies and biographies have equated leadership with the work of executives at the top of organizations, whether in government, the military, business, or education. Likewise, leadership in colleges and universities has been associated with presidents who have left a distinctive imprint on their institutions and on higher education. Individuals who come to mind include Charles William Eliot of Harvard, Robert Maynard Hutchins of the University of Chicago, Clark Kerr of the University of California, and the Reverend Theodore Hesburgh of the University of Notre Dame.

The characteristics and qualities of effective college presidents have been identified by a number of studies (Kerr, 1984; Gilley, 1985). One recent study (Fisher, Tack, and Wheeler, 1988) concludes that the traditional "Mr. Chips" stereotype of college presidents should be revised; instead, effective presidents emerge as "strong action-oriented visionaries who act out of a kind of educated intuition" (p. ix).

Another type of research and analysis of leadership in higher education has focused on the culture of leadership. Analyzing the culture of higher education, Birnbaum (1988) identifies the collegial, bureaucratic, political, and organized anarchy models of organization, and he offers views on their integration. His work acknowledges the many and varied actors who affect how institutions are governed and led. Case-study research offers insights into the collegiate culture and identifies the need for different and expanded leadership strategies (Chaffee and Tierney, 1988). As some have noted, these strategies will have to involve many others besides the president. Kauffman (1987) notes the "need for new studies in leadership that involve the behavior of more than one individual, because campus leadership today involves more than a president. It involves a governing board, senior officers of administration, faculty and student leaders, and a structure and process of governance that encourages satisfaction and productive effort. The relationships among all these factors need to be carefully explored" (p. 447).

Over the past few decades, astute observers of higher education have called on student personnel professionals to be key players on campus leadership teams as institutions face the challenges of the future. These challenges include reforming the undergraduate curriculum, responding to diversity, shaping institutional values, and integrating student affairs and academic affairs (Brown, 1972; Garland, 1985; Boyer, 1987). Studies on the leadership roles of student affairs and academic services professionals are relatively few in number, however. Of almost six hundred annotated studies of higher education governance, management, and leadership, only five are identified with student affairs (Peterson and

Mets, 1987). Leadership is essential to the creative improvement of services and programs for our increasingly diverse student populations. Nevertheless, leadership in student services must also go beyond improvement of direct services, to bring about an impact on larger issues of institutional concern. With their perspectives, priorities, commitments, and experiences, student personnel professionals are well equipped to grapple with the challenges currently facing higher education. If those of us in the profession are to assume roles of greater impact, we will need to draw strength from our heritage, understand contemporary issues, and look within to document and learn from current exemplary leaders.

This chapter provides a backdrop to our study of effective leadership in student affairs. It traces the heritage of the profession and highlights the complex nature of governance and leadership in modern higher education. It also delineates how leadership in student services is presented in the literature. Finally, it describes a method of study that enables exemplary leaders to share their experiences with and their perspectives on the complex practice of the student affairs profession. This chapter sets the stage for all the remaining chapters, which feature the voices of today's exemplary practitioners.

Heritage

The student affairs profession has its roots in Colonial times, when the responsibilities we now associate with the profession were assumed by faculty members, who frequently performed these duties while in residence with students (Rudolph, 1962). The most obvious roles were counselor, adviser, teacher, tutor, and disciplinarian. As institutions expanded in size and complexity, they began to differentiate instructional and supportive services more clearly. As more roles in supportive services evolved, the seeds of a broadly defined student personnel profession were sown.

As the profession grew, key leaders emerged, including some pioneering deans in the late nineteenth and early twentieth centuries, who significantly influenced their institutions

and the development of the profession. In 1889, E. H. Griffin
of Johns Hopkins University was appointed, as the first "chief
of the faculty advisers," to counsel and advise students
(Mueller, 1961; Rudolph, 1962). The beginning of a formal
student affairs program is identified with the appointment of
Dean LaBaron Briggs at Harvard in 1890 (Shaffer, 1987). By
the early twentieth century, some individuals (for example,
C. S. Yoakum) were clearly advocating separate and distinct
student affairs departments (Saddlemire and Rentz, 1986).
Although such departments were limited in the scope of their
responsibilities, their establishment was significant. It recognized that student services was a separate area of expertise
within higher education.

     Many in the student personnel field point to a pivotal
event in the development of the profession: the publication of
The Student Personnel Point of View (American Council on
Education, 1937). A revised edition appeared in 1949. Together, these landmark statements served as the foundation of
the student affairs profession by elaborating philosophical
underpinnings, by defining roles, and by identifying areas of
responsibility, as well as administrative relationships. The
wonder of these documents is that they are simultaneously
inspirational and pragmatic; they affirm the nobility of service to the profession, to institutions, and to students.

     As the profession developed, there were additional con-
tributions to philosophical perspectives and role definitions.
In particular Tomorrow's Higher Education (T.H.E.) Project,
conceived by the American College Personnel Association in
1968, resulted in documents that affirmed the importance of
student development to all areas of the educational enterprise
(Brown, 1972) and called for relevant strategies in teaching,
consultation, and environmental management (Miller and
Prince, 1976). The Commission on Professional Development
of the Council of Student Personnel Associations in Higher
Education also affirmed the centrality of human development
and produced a competence-based curriculum for graduate
preparation programs. The curriculum stressed roles for student development specialists as administrators, consultants,

and instructors. In 1987, the fiftieth anniversary of the original publication of *The Student Personnel Point of View*, the same spirit informed *A Perspective on Student Affairs* (National Association of Student Personnel Administrators, 1987). This document enumerates the major assumptions and beliefs that undergird professional practice, as well as the multiple roles for professionals in student affairs.

By contrast with the broad, integrative roles conceived for the profession, a countervailing movement was also under way. The profession evolved into a compendium of specialty areas (residence life, judicial programs, campus activities, admissions), and many developed their own professional organizations, journals, and bodies of literature. The development of all these specialty areas reflects the evolution of the profession as represented by its practitioners' increased need for specialized knowledge and for association with others having similar responsibilities. This development has been useful and necessary, but it has also fragmented the profession. Nevertheless, such fragmentation is probably natural and inevitable in a complex system that compels its participants to strive continually for improvement in the delivery of educational programs and services. Moreover, this specialization has been vital to the development of the profession.

It is now time to seek once again a perspective on what is still special and unique about our overall profession, as *The Student Personnel Point of View* did in 1937 and 1949. This attempt at "centering" our profession will be particularly important for the challenges of the 1990s.

The evolving student services profession has been true to the core values of our heritage. These core values include viewing each student as a unique individual, recognizing the educational importance of out-of-class activities, valuing a sense of community, and living out an ethic of service. These values informed the practice of the profession's pioneers and the words of the profession's first formal documents.

Recently, these values were also reflected in a project that captures the voices of some of our early exemplary leaders: the American College Personnel Association Generativity

Project, 1983–1988. A series of taped interviews with these leaders includes conversations with Esther Lloyd-Jones, Robert H. (Bob) Shaffer, and C. Gilbert Wrenn. These interviews give us perspectives on our heritage and on the values that have remained at the core of the student services profession throughout its evolution.

In her interview, Esther Lloyd-Jones, who helped write both versions of *The Student Personnel Point of View*, names the values of student personnel as "the importance of the individual, the respect for community, and the recognition of the campus as a number of intersecting communities." Within that conceptual framework, she stresses the importance of the profession's fostering leadership opportunities among students. C. Gilbert Wrenn, who also helped craft those documents, echoes many of Esther Lloyd-Jones's comments in his interview. His career has exemplified the power of caring, and so it is not surprising to hear him say that the essence of the profession is "the focus on the development of the student as a person." Recalling the historic documents, he says, "We wrote the statement[s] for ourselves." His remarks reflect the profession's underlying ethic of care.

Defining our responsibilities, Robert Shaffer calls on the profession to help faculty members see that "we are doing a job complementary to their work as educators." Although they recognized the distinctive nature of the profession, our early leaders also recognized the importance of integrating our role into the larger campus community and elevating student service and advocacy to a primary role in institutions. Shaffer affirms the importance of the profession, exhorting us to foster an "image" of student personnel as representing a positive educational force rather than a custodial, supportive service.

As the profession evolves from its unique heritage, it encompasses more differentiated roles, which are nevertheless forged through common commitments (to the individual, to development of the whole person, to recognition of community responsibilities) and an essential underlying ethic of care. Our core values continue to define the practice of our profession.

Governance and Leadership in Higher Education

Many observers of higher education draw attention to the difficulty of leading and governing our modern institutions. Keller (1983) describes in great detail the progressive decline in institutional decision making and the resulting decline in the quality of education. Others (Boyer, 1987; Garland, 1985) provide us with cogent analyses of our problems, pointing out the incoherence of curricula, the ineffectiveness of extracurricular programs, the disenchantment of faculty members, and the detached attitudes of students. The ultimate outcome of these developments has been the demoralization of our internal and external constituents and the devaluation of the undergraduate degree.

Amid this widely acknowledged crisis in higher education, thoughtful critics and blue-ribbon panels implore college presidents and other institutional administrators to assume leadership, take risks, and demonstrate initiative and imagination (Bennett, 1985; Association of American Colleges, 1985). It is important to note, however, that we call on major institutional leaders to demonstrate leadership in the unique culture of higher education, where administration is viewed as a necessary evil that supports the central mission of the institution, teaching and learning (Green, 1988).

The role of faculty members in decision making is truly unique. It helps distinguish institutions of higher education from all other organizations and sometimes compounds problems of leadership and decision making. The American Association of University Professors (1984) affirms the authority of faculty members and the importance of institutional leaders' carrying out their will. Major administrators who get too far ahead of the faculty can find themselves stranded, without support or respect. The same fate can befall administrators who fail to manage their areas competently and with a clear vision of how the function, program, or service fits in with current institutional priorities. Maintaining the precarious balance between carrying out the will of the faculty and asserting vigorous, visionary leadership is a dilemma peculiar to institutions of higher education.

Given the unique culture of higher education, it is easy to see why traditional theories of leadership and governance do not adequately explain institutions' current functioning or prescribe appropriate courses of action for current and aspiring administrative leaders. We do need leaders who understand the traditional leadership theories, but they must also understand the peculiar sociological phenomena of decision making in higher education. These are partly explained by cultural and symbolic theories; but they are also, in good measure, challenges peculiar to higher education and the current era. If student services administrators are to be successful in asserting leadership, they must clearly understand the channels for shaping institutional opinions and decisions.

Leadership and the Literature of the Profession

In considering how student services professionals can provide institutional leadership in the modern era, it seems logical to turn to the literature on leadership in higher education. While this work has been a valuable contribution, it emphasizes the role of the president and does not present a complete perspective. Some sources (Boyer, 1987; Garland, 1985; Green, 1988; Carnegie Foundation for the Advancement of Teaching, 1990) acknowledge that leadership on the part of others, specifically on the part of student and academic services professionals, will be important in maintaining and improving the quality of institutions. The Carnegie Foundation for the Advancement of Teaching (1990) challenges student affairs professionals to be purposeful, open, just, disciplined, caring, and celebratory in helping improve the sense of community on campuses. Green (1988) calls for shared leadership and for the development of leaders throughout institutions. Garland (1985) urges the student affairs profession to provide leadership by extending some current roles and assuming new ones. Chief among these will be that of "integrator"—someone who can burrow into the institution and promote its coherence. The message is clear: student services professionals need to change the perception, all too common, that they are "estranged from the vital functions of the academic enterprise" and that they are "indispensable, but peripheral" (Fenske, 1980).

There is a strong call for leadership in our profession, but the literature exploring this concept is scant. It focuses primarily on career pathways (Kuh, Evans, and Duke, 1983; Rickard, 1985; Sagaria, 1988) and on the administration and management of programs and services (Delworth, Hanson, and Associates, 1980, 1989; Barr, Keating, and Associates, 1985; Upcraft and Barr, 1988; Sandeen, 1991). These works offer valuable knowledge and perspectives and are tools for student services administrators who want to exert institutional leadership. Insights into how these tools can be used effectively are found in Appleton, Briggs, and Rhatigan (1978). This classic naturalistic study, conducted almost fifteen years ago, sets forth the views of eight chief student affairs officers who were also presidents of the National Association of Student Personnel Administrators (NASPA). The study discusses how the leadership styles of the eight former NASPA presidents contributed to their effectiveness.

The literature on leadership in student and academic services includes valuable information for the professional seeking ways to assume a stronger leadership role. Much of this literature seems fragmented, however, separating functional roles from leadership and viewing style as independent of situation. Moreover, no comprehensive study of leadership has used a broad cross section of leaders working in a variety of student services roles and functions.

A Qualitative Study of Effective Leaders

With this book, we hope to contribute to the literature on leadership in student services by examining leadership in action and exploring the congruence of our respondents' perspectives with those expressed in the literature. The research on which this book is based reflects a qualitative approach to effective leadership. The research design was influenced by Peters and Waterman (1982), Peters and Austin (1985), Bennis and Nanus (1985), and Kouzes and Posner (1987). By definition, this is a qualitative rather than a quantitative study. Rather than counting traits, behaviors, or outcomes, this study involves in-depth examination of the characteristics, viewpoints, ideas, challenges, and struggles of a group of people identified as leaders by their peers in student services. This type of study can reveal elements of the leadership experience inaccessible to quantitative methods (Caple, 1991).

This study also represents a departure from traditional leadership studies, and it reflects what Kuh, Whitt, and Shedd (1987) characterize as a shift from a conventional paradigm to an emergent one. We sought information from new and different angles, basing our work on an assumption adapted from Clark (1985): that the complex question of leadership in student services demands a "new story" that "will generate deeper and richer understandings" (p. 17). For some scholars, responding to this demand involves the use of qualitative research methods; Brown (1988a) touches on the need for such new understanding when he states that "solid experimental research must be balanced with good qualitative studies" (p. 99), and Coles (1989) stresses how much can be learned from careful listening to and analysis of stories.

Qualitative research entails the assessment of respondents' opinions and ideas from the vantage point of an *emergent paradigm*. Many of the characteristics of emerging paradigms identified by Kuh, Whitt, and Shedd (1987) are applicable:

- Events are presented through the respondents' experience, values, and expectations.
- Order is seen as being created through networks of mutual influence and constraint.
- Some degree of ambiguity and disorder is expected, valued, and exploited.
- Events are understood as being generated by complex reciprocal processes that blur distinctions between cause and effect.

In telling this "new story" about leadership in student services, we examine issues and events through leaders' experiences. We acknowledge and value the complexity and mutuality of relationships, and we recognize that leadership in higher education is made up of complex and sometimes ambiguous reciprocal processes. In this way, we use an emergent paradigm, one that is revealed through the perspectives of our respondents.

We asked leaders a series of open-ended questions (see Resource C), and they shared their opinions, ideas, accomplishments, and frustrations. Their responses were analyzed by theme and topic and are presented in this book.

Identifying Leaders

During 1988 and 1989, effective leaders were identified by a process of peer nomination. We were looking for chief student affairs officers and for directors of admissions, career development and placement, cooperative education, commuter affairs, counseling, financial aid, international education, judicial affairs, learning centers, minority affairs, orientation, police and public safety, the registrar's office, residential life, student health, student activities, and student unions. If the campus leader in a particular functional area had the title of associate or assistant director, he or she was included in the group of directors. Nominations were solicited from university presidents who had served as chief student affairs officers, graduate faculty members who had served as chief student affairs officers, and leaders of professional associations. Chief student affairs officers who were nominated by the first three groups were also given the option of nominating directors of student and academic services, with no more than two nominees from their own campuses permitted. Nominating faculty members were chosen in a way that ensured regional balance, with no more than two from the same institution. (See Resource A.)

Resource B lists the respondents alphabetically, including their institutional affiliations and positions. Some respon-

changed jobs over the course of the study; current status precedes job title and institution at the time of nomination.

The nominators were asked to identify individuals who had earned a reputation for effectiveness in leadership on their campuses. The primary consideration was leadership on campus, in contrast to leadership in professional associations. Effective leadership was operationally defined as "doing the right things" (Bennis and Nanus, 1985; Cameron, 1985). Nominees were to have been in their current positions for a minimum of five years or in similar positions at a similar level for five years before having assumed their current positions. (The criterion of five years was intended to strengthen the credibility of the nominations.)

Gathering Responses

Chief student affairs officers and directors were informed of their nominations in writing and were invited to answer the open-ended questions. These were based on a review of the leadership literature and on consultation with acknowledged leaders who were also nominators. The questions concerned attributes, leadership skills, leadership approaches, risks, challenges, obstacles to success, theory, philosophy, values, roles, relationships, identity, race relations, diversity, student and campus crises, and institutional climate (see Resource C).

Several individuals received multiple nominations, but even a single nomination qualified an individual to participate in the study. Nominees were given the option of responding anonymously or being quoted and identified by their titles and institutional affiliations. After they responded to the open-ended questions, the participants completed a profile questionnaire. The questionnaire included items on gender, race, age, institutional affiliation, academic degrees, institutions where academic degrees were earned, number of years in current position, number of years in higher education, types of full-time positions in higher education, academic affiliations, publications, and professional associations and activities. The results are shown in Resource D.

Analyzing the Responses

Since this study used qualitative analysis methods, answers to questions were subjected to inductive data analysis, which allows themes to emerge from results of an inquiry. In this method, raw information is put into subsuming categories that define organization of the results (Lincoln and Guba, 1985). What emerges generally is a set of themes or patterns of perceptions and actions (Patton, 1991). Interpretive techniques attempt to come to terms with the meanings, not the frequency, of data items (Whitt, 1991). In the chapters that follow, representative quotations will be presented, rather than all comments on a particular topic.

Results

This study presents a unique and intimate view of exemplary leaders in student and academic services. Their perspectives are presented in their own words. What emerges is a crystallization of what it takes to be an effective and even exemplary leader in student and academic services. The following topics emerged:

1. Elements necessary to leadership in the profession (attributes, skills, and institutional conditions)
2. Relationships essential to success, including those with students, faculty members, staff people, and supervisors
3. Challenges that test our ability to focus on campus crises, day-to-day dilemmas, and quandaries about identity
4. The ethic of care, the essential ingredient of success as a leader in academic and student services

PART ONE

Essential Elements of Effective Leadership

CHAPTER TWO

Personal Attributes Associated with Success

At the very core of exemplary leadership is the possession of particular attributes. Tom Wolfe, characterizing the early test pilots and seven Mercury astronauts, talked about attributes as "the right stuff"—"an amalgam of stamina, guts, fast neural synapses and old-fashioned hell raising" (Wolfe, 1980, p. 368). What is the "right stuff" for professionals in student and academic services? Are there identifiable personal attributes characteristic of effective leaders in student and academic services? This chapter reveals the personal attributes that characterize effective leaders in student affairs. Possession of these attributes is not enough to guarantee professional success, but their absence is quite certainly a major deterrent. The voices of effective leaders, as well as the literature on leadership in business, industry, and higher education, are incorporated into our examination of personal attributes.

Various studies document the difficulty of identifying universal traits of successful leaders (Stogdill, 1948; Bass, 1981;

Bass and Stogdill, 1990; Yukl, 1981, 1989). Bass and Stogdill (1990) say, "There is no overall comprehensive theory of the personality of leaders. Nonetheless, evidence abounds about particular patterns of determination, persistence, self-confidence, and ego strength" (p. 87).

Drawing on these studies, Gardner (1990) summarizes the attributes of leaders as follows: intelligence and judgment-in-action; willingness to accept responsibilities; task competence; understanding of followers and constituents and their needs; skill in dealing with people; the need to achieve; the capacity to motivate; courage, resolution, and steadiness, the capacity to win trust and hold it; the capacity to manage, decide, and set priorities; confidence; ascendance, dominance, and assertiveness; and adaptability and flexibility of approach. These studies support the situational nature of leadership, affirm the need to turn to experts in higher education, and provide reference points for the present study of effective leaders in student services.

Attributes of Effective Leaders

The effective leaders surveyed for our study identify three constellations of attributes and related personal qualities that have contributed to their success:

- *Integrity,* involving trust, honesty, loyalty, courage, and risk taking
- *Commitment,* evidenced by a positive attitude toward working with students, enthusiasm, joy, optimism, and passion for student services work
- *Tenacity,* focusing on a strong work ethic, perseverance, patience, and follow-through

Integrity

For the leaders surveyed for this study, integrity includes clear values—a definitive sense of right and wrong, and firmly honored standards of conduct. Beyond this core, it also includes the exercise of personal values, the practice of a coherent philosophy of education, and commitment to the people and to the institutions served. With strong core values and the courage to take risks, effective leaders fulfill their responsibilities with integrity. They act on the basis of their strongly held values. Although some aspects of leadership have been described as situational, integrity stays constant, regardless of the circumstances.

The importance of integrity has been widely noted. Bennis (1989b) affirms the importance of integrity and defines it as "standards of moral and intellectual honesty on which our conduct is based" (p. 117). As a basic ingredient of leadership, integrity includes three essential parts: self-knowledge, candor, and maturity (Bennis, 1989a). Heyns (1973) identifies honesty, integrity, compassion, and cooperation as essential leadership traits. Integrity has been identified by 1,500 managers as the personal trait or characteristic most admired in a supervisor (Kouzes and Posner, 1987, p. 16). Drawing on a variety of sources, Srivastva and Associates (1988) go beyond definitions and have derived "ten commandments of executive integrity": "telling the truth; obeying the law; reducing ambiguity; showing concern for others; accepting responsibility for the growth and nurturing of subordinates; practicing participation, not paternalism; providing freedom from corrupting influences; always acting; providing consistency across cases; and providing consistency between values and actions" (pp. 126–127).

The value and importance of integrity have also been noted in the student affairs literature. Writing more than a quarter of a century ago on the changing roles of student personnel deans, Thrash (1965) identified four important personal qualities: integrity, intelligence, openness, and commitment. Integrity reappears in a landmark study of eight NASPA presidents, in which Appleton, Briggs, and Rhatigan (1978) found that integrity is a common quality among chief student affairs officers, with frequent references to "truthfulness, straight talk, and no bluffing" (p. 72). Integrity has been identified by Young (1991) as an essential value and personal quality in student affairs practice and education. Viewing student affairs as playing the role of "institutional conscience," Barr (1987) says that student affairs has a "special responsibility to raise questions of fairness, equity, honesty, and responsibilities during policy formation and crisis intervention" (p. 3). Knefelkamp (1989) has called on the profession to take strong stands and to view integrity as a conviction.

The subjects of this study spoke eloquently about the importance of integrity. William Butler, vice-president for student affairs for over a quarter of a century at the University of Miami and a student affairs administrator for over forty years, reflects as follows: "To survive over the years as a senior administrator in several major universities is by no means an easy task. To survive nearly forty years in administration with perceived integrity [among] one's colleagues and others is a far greater accomplishment. Integrity in student services emanates from one's philosophy of higher education. I believe that a central tenet in that philosophy should be that students are essential partners in the university's decision-making processes, along with faculty and administration."

Other institutional leaders surveyed for this study emphasize the idea that integrity is paramount among attributes and is a cornerstone of their work. Donald Adams, vice-president for enrollment management and student life at Drake University and a chief student affairs officer for over twenty consecutive years, speaks with conviction about the importance of personal and professional integrity: "As administrators, we can all put together beautiful plans and programs, be highly respected for the staff members we recruit, organize fine staff development programs, and evaluate with the best. However, if we do not have personal and professional respect or integrity, then our reputations, on campus as well as off campus, will never allow us to be successful. Somehow, some way, every chief student affairs administrator must come to grips with a standard of integrity that does not allow other people to be abused or used and must continue to learn how to listen and act on what he or she hears."

Brigida Knauer, dean of students at Occidental College, shares the belief that "integrity is the most important personal quality for a dean of students to possess. Clearly, one wouldn't achieve that level of responsibility without a lot of other things being in place, including effective leadership, successful administrative skills, understanding the mission of both the job and the institution, and the ability to move shared goals forward. With all those obvious things, it seems to me that without integrity one has nothing. In order to be an effective role model for students, in order to be an effective role model for colleagues, integrity is paramount. In my case, it allows me to be outspoken in general and to serve as an advocate for students and for student affairs on campus."

Integrity enables leaders to assume other important roles as well. Ruth Jass, registrar emeritus of Bradley University, notes the importance integrity plays in one's ability to lead and to serve as an advocate: "Only when my integrity is not in question can I expect others to follow my lead. Honesty is the foundation on which trust is built. It is only in an atmosphere of trust that my perceptions will be valued as I speak out in forums on campus and within my spheres of influence in the community of higher education and in the greater society. Management with honor is an absolute necessity for a leader, and I as a manager and leader must set the example for the staff."

As noted above, integrity enables leaders to assume the role of advocate, and it also enables leaders to have a firm foundation for building trusting relationships. Tom Thielen, vice-president for student affairs at Iowa State University, says, "Integrity of relationships will allow you to project your messages with succinctness and clarity. Your words and your actions will be better understood when you say what you mean and mean what you say. Likewise, this clarity will model for others the choice of giving clearer messages to you. Integrity is the building block of trust."

Trust and Honesty

Trust and honesty are related to integrity. They are key elements of credibility. Honesty has been identified in numerous studies as the top-ranked quality in expectations of leaders and followers (Kouzes, 1989). Whetten and Cameron (1985) note that trust and fairness are characteristics of effective administrators. Effective college presidents are described as being trusting and trustworthy (Fisher, Tack, and Wheeler, 1988). Gardner (1990) identifies "fairness" and "steadiness" as essential prerequisites for leaders' winning the trust of constituents. Writing about student affairs professionals, Sandeen (1991) says, "It is critical to be honest all the time, on every issue or problem" (p. 44).

The leaders surveyed for this study affirm the importance of trust and honesty. They believe that trust and honesty are inextricably related to integrity. Robert Etheridge, vice-president emeritus for student affairs at Miami University, speaks directly of this link: "Integrity, coupled with candid honesty, has been most helpful in meeting crises or stating expectations. As the trite old expression goes, you never have to remember what you said when you tell the truth."

James Quann, registrar and director of student information systems at the University of California, Santa Cruz, also says that "integrity is of utmost importance. We must be honest and straightforward in everything we do—honest with students, honest with staff members, and direct and honest with our faculty, including deans and unit heads. Straightforwardness must also be of high value. As keepers of the academic keys to the university, and as administrators in charge of implementing and interpreting the rules and policies laid down by the faculty, we must also be straightforward in our responses. Even when our decision is no, we must be honest and straight with our answer. It is easy to answer a tough question when the answer is yes, but if it is not, we must be kind, courteous and empathetic—but honest and straightforward, too." Quann and other leaders surveyed for this study have emphasized that trust, honesty, and integrity are not situational characteristics but are universal to all situations.

Charles Renneisen, vice-chancellor for student affairs at the University of Tennessee, Chattanooga, affirms the relationship of integrity to honesty and trust: "Integrity is the single most essential quality. A strong reputation of trust and honesty will weather the many storms and crises a dean must endure." Timothy Sheridan, director of student judicial programs at Western Illinois University, talks about how integrity extends beyond the leader: "I expect thorough, professional-quality work. I expect my staff to uphold the integrity of the office and its operations. I invest trust in my staff members and challenge them to be confident in their decision making." William Rodgers, former director of financial aid at the University of South Alabama, concurs: "I believe that an organization which can employ people of integrity and intelligence is well on the way to success."

Loyalty

Loyalty is important, regardless of one's level or position in student or academic services, and it is an attribute essential to the success of institutional leaders. Loyalty involves institutions as well as individuals. It is evident from the comments of the leaders surveyed for this study that loyalty to supervisors and to employing institutions is absolutely essential to success. This finding is borne out by a study of eight former NASPA presidents, who stress the critical importance of institutional loyalty (Appleton, Briggs, and Rhatigan, 1978). DiBrito (1990) has conducted a naturalistic study of interpersonal loyalty between chief student affairs officers and their superiors and subordinates at four institutions, finding that loyalty includes the personal attributes of honesty, respect, and trust. The concept of loyalty encompasses several dichotomies: it can be both emotional and rational, it can be given willingly or unwillingly, and it can be earned or automatic. Loyalty can also be situational, dependent on professional competence and on the position and personal competence of the individuals involved.

    Tim Gallineau, vice-president for student development at Saint Bonaventure University, defines demonstrated loyalty to the organization as "constant behavior intended to build and not tear down the organization." For successful leaders, constructive, positive attitudes and behavior extend beyond organizations and beyond student affairs. Joel Rudy, dean of students at Ohio University, expresses this idea when he articulates loyalty as a shared responsibility, one that has at its heart "an institutional perspective versus a division or departmental perspective on administration of the institution." He says, "I live this in my work with all staff members and students and try to convey my belief that we all participate somewhat equally in the success of the total institution. Success of an individual area at the expense of, or in neglect of, another area, including people, detracts from, if it doesn't inhibit, the success of the total institutional mission. This is accomplished through compromise, caring, and communication."

Identifying loyalty as contributing to her success, Marsha Duncan, vice-president for student affairs at Lehigh University, emphasizes the importance of loyalty to one's supervisor: "If a chief does not genuinely feel intense loyalty to the president, the institution, and the staff, then that chief needs to change institutions. We do serve at the pleasure of the president, and that means many things—delivering in our jobs, being advocates for the institution, carrying out the goals of the institution, protecting the president, and, in fact, making him or her look good!" It is important to note that loyalty to a person or to an institution does not mean unconditional agreement. As Duncan says, "Loyalty must include honesty, openness, and a willingness to fight battles with doors closed; then—win, lose, or draw—it means providing full support for the final decision." This statement raises the idea that one element of loyalty is honesty with one's supervisor. The effective leader provides his or her supervisor with his or her best thinking about an issue, even when it is in disagreement with the supervisor or others. After his or her opinion has been aired and considered, however, the effective leader supports the final decision.

Courage and Risk Taking

If student services professionals have integrity and honesty, what else is necessary? Richard Correnti, vice-president for student affairs at Florida International University, names honesty and integrity as essential but adds courage as another important attribute: "Honesty and integrity go hand in hand and must be exhibited at all times. One must work harder than normally expected and maintain ethical standards which are beyond reproach. This means not playing games with people, not being solely concerned with personal reward, and not cutting corners. In my experience, courage is also a very important quality for administrators. Most people can readily distinguish between right and wrong, but it is not always easy to have the courage to do what is right. Often this requires disagreement, going against the flow, or confronting another individual—a student, a staff member, a peer, or a supervisor. It also requires making tough decisions, as well as routine ones. Anyone can make popular decisions; making the unpopular ones and convincing others that they are correct is what separates the outstanding from the average administrator." Claire Swann, director of admissions at the University of Georgia, identifies courage as the single most important personal quality that has contributed to her success, characterizing it as "courage to be aggressive with internal publics."

Both Correnti and Swann acknowledge the confrontational aspects of courageous behavior, and effective leaders do realize that courage may have consequences. Thomas Dutton, former vice-chancellor for student affairs at the University of California, Davis, speaks poignantly about these consequences: "To accomplish a difficult and challenging task not only requires persistence and good strategy and tactics but oftentimes courage to face obstacles, criticism, and threat of failure, and even ridicule. The more complex and emotional the problem, the more likely it is that there will be strongly held views on all sides of the issue. It takes considerable courage to address such problems, because of the consequences— the inevitable pain and suffering in successful or unsuccessful pursuit of appropriate solutions."

Courage also affects the nature and intensity of relationships with staff members. Kitty Arnold, director of career and placement services at the University of Notre Dame, suggests that courage and risk taking are important qualities in establishing caring relationships with staff members: "One must have the courage to become involved, to some degree, in other people's lives—to take the risk of sharing their triumphs, their failures, their blue moods, and their antics. You, not just they, have to be willing to feel something in order to have a shared mission."

What these leaders have to say about courage is reaffirmed by others outside our field. Integrity involves having the courage of one's convictions: "To live with integrity in our highly pluralistic and multivalent society . . . takes courage" (Srivastva and Associates, 1988, p. 169). Given the challenge of diversity facing institutions of higher education, successful leaders will need integrity and courage.

Astin and Scherrei's profile (1980) of chief student affairs administrators notes that they place a high value on taking risks. The leaders surveyed for this study agree, asserting that an important dimension of courage is risk taking. As a personal quality essential to running an organization, the willingness to take risks characterizes ninety top national leaders (Bennis and Nanus, 1985). The willingness to take risks is one of the defining characteristics of an administrator's effectiveness in higher education (Whetten and Cameron, 1985).

Randall Powell, assistant dean and director of placement at Indiana University's School of Business, says, "The single personal quality most important to my success has been my willingness to take risks for creative projects in the risk-averse environment of student services. I have been supported by administrators who were also willing to risk their reputations on some of my ideas." William Thomas, Jr., vice-president for student affairs for over twenty years at the University of Maryland, College Park, agrees as he reflects on the importance of courage: "One thing which seems to make a difference is when you have enough courage to call things for what they are, or to risk your reputation, or to invest a lot and count on the outcome to be good."

Richard Keeling, director of the Department of Student

Health at the University of Virginia, envisions a better future, which compels him to take risks. He emphasizes how "thinking in macro terms has allowed me to look past the conflicts and controversies of the moment, as long as I felt secure in my assessment that what I planned or worked on was an effective strategy in the long run. On the positive side, my macro point of view provides a substantial foundation for my taking some risks in my work. Looking at the big picture of the greater significance of things, I often conclude that some gambles in the current moment will pay off in the long haul, although they may create some temporary difficulties, uncertainties, or conflicts. A good example is the initial work done by my Task Force on AIDS for the American College Health Association [ACHA]. When we sent out our initial set of policy recommendations, in December 1985, we took a considerable risk that our work would be seen as not credible, or as too far beyond what other people were thinking. We knew that the release of our preliminary and general statements on institutional responses to AIDS would cause some controversies, and it did. However, there was a clear payoff—and not only for ACHA, but also for colleges, universities, students, and the national effort to provide reasonable responses to HIV/AIDS. In taking these risks, I am willing to seize opportunities, measure the probabilities of success or failure, and make relatively fast decisions." Keeling also asserts his willingness to endure criticism if he believes that the benefits will be worth it.

Risk-taking behavior that puts administrators on the cutting edge of the profession has costs. As Keeling says, "My macro point of view is not without negative effects, of course. The people I work with may see me as insufficiently involved in the day-to-day management and life of our health center, and my habit of looking at the long-run picture may make me appear to be insensitive to the pain of conflicts in the present. I try to be careful not to let my eagerness to keep moving toward a better world cause a much worse world for individual colleagues at the current time. I have to deal with the occasional frustration of a friend, colleague, or staff member who thinks my preoccupation with the forest leads me to pay insufficient attention to some of the trees. As time has passed, I believe, I have learned to balance these needs more effectively."

Debra Sivertson, director of student health services at the University of Maryland, Baltimore County, affirms the importance of the goals of risk-taking behavior: "As a risk taker, I have continually tried to be out in front in many areas in my field. It is important to be able to recognize the need for change—not just for the sake of change, but also to be able to provide the best care for students." As Sivertson points out, risk taking is not an end in itself; it is always related to the improvement of a program, service, or situation.

Risk taking and change often involve gaining the approval, cooperation, and support of colleagues, so that all may benefit. Sivertson says, "By recognizing such areas of importance as skill-based peer prevention programs for all areas, HIV disease-prevention education, other sexually transmitted diseases, stress, nutrition, health insurance issues, immunization issues, and many diverse groups' needs in college health services, I have been able to effectively change the system, with staff members, students, and faculty involved, so that the change process has been supported and individuals feel good about the changes."

As Keeling and Sivertson indicate, risk taking requires expertise and vision. It also requires us to trust those around us. "I am willing to take risks," says Margaret Bridwell, director of the Student Health Center at the University of Maryland, College Park. "You need to know what you are talking about and be willing to explain and discuss, never talking down to anyone." She adds, "You need confidence in yourself, but respect for others."

Obviously, integrity is paramount in the successful provision of student and academic services. As leaders gain and exhibit trust and loyalty, they find the courage to take risks and improve their institutions for those they serve.

Commitment

Virtually all the institutional leaders surveyed for this study have professed commitment to their work. Commitment evolves from enjoyment of the work, an optimistic attitude toward possibilities and outcomes, and a firm conviction of the importance of student services work. These traits combine to produce commitment.

Positive Attitude Toward Working with Students

Leaders affirm that working with students is the centerpiece of their commitment. Francine Madrey, vice-president for student affairs at Johnson C. Smith University, says she is "energized by [students'] enthusiasm and support. I find it refreshing to work around young people on a day-to-day basis, for one is constantly learning. As they call upon us to become more accountable, they encourage and require us to grow along with them."

Other leaders substantiate the impression of energy derived from interactions with students. Samuel Sadler, vice-president for student affairs at the College of William and Mary, says, "By far, I am happiest when I am working one-on-one with a student. Nothing compares with the excitement and satisfaction I derive from talking through a concern with a student or being of help in some other way. I find myself energized by these relationships, and they constantly provide the focus I need for my work. As my responsibilities have increased over the years, I have been careful to build into every day some opportunity for student contact."

Dorothy Anderson, dean of students at Susquehanna University, also affirms the importance of student contact. She says that she derives "a deep and abiding joy from participating in and assisting with the growth, development, and education of college students. Without that, many aspects of the dean's job would be far too frustrating to stand."

Their roles in working with students differ dramatically, but the theme of service characterizes the essence of these leaders' commitment to their work. This is evident in the perspective of Herman Kissiah, dean of students at Lafayette College: "I entered this profession, I believe, because I felt that I could help students reach more of their potential as young men and young women. I came from a family and a church tradition that valued service and commitment to others. I inherited that tradition and became a part of it, and it of me. While my responsibilities have changed significantly, from my days sitting in a college residence hall and talking with a couple of freshmen to my work as dean of students today, I do believe that my motivation has always been service." It is important to note that this commitment to service extends to all levels, from the front line to the upper levels of the administration.

Enthusiasm and Joy

Enjoyment of student contact is also mentioned by leaders in every size and type of institution. Stanley Levy, vice-chancellor for student affairs at the University of Illinois, an institution with an enrollment of over twenty thousand, says, "There is no doubt in my mind that the role I enjoy the most is work with students. In almost thirty years in this profession, there have been only a half-dozen students whom I really have not liked, have not wanted to deal with, and would do my very best to avoid at all costs. What got me into the business in the first place—the opportunity to observe, participate in, and occasionally influence the growth of young people— is what keeps me going."

In addition to enjoying their work with students, exemplary leaders maintain a positive attitude toward their work and toward the future. "I don't know whether I'm in student services because I'm an optimist or I'm an optimist because I'm in student services," remarks Thomas Coyne, former vice-president for student services at Western Michigan University, now retired. "I do know that I could not have survived these past twenty years without this positive attitude, enhanced by the outstanding colleagues with whom I have been fortunate to be associated. This is a wonderful profession. The students with whom we deal are, in the vast majority, marvelous young men and women. They stimulate, excite, irritate, and challenge. The problems are varied, and just about the time we feel everything is quiet and the place is dull, all hell breaks loose. The juices start to flow, decisions need to be made; you feel alive and of service to people."

A positive attitude and enthusiasm have also been identified as important qualities of effective leaders in the "excellence" literature. Being "positive" and being "optimistic" are attributes of successful middle- and senior-level leaders in public and private organizations (Kouzes and Posner, 1987). Peters and Austin (1985) find that "pride in one's organization and enthusiasm for its works" are the two most important basics of managerial success (p. 16).

As Nikos Kazantzakis wrote in *Zorba the Greek* (1964), "Zorba sees everything every day as if for the first time" (p. 6). Leaders in the profession share a similar attitude. Alice Manicur, vice-president for student and educational services at Frostburg State University, offers a personal glimpse of her Zorba-like enthusiasm for her work: "I like what I do. I do not find myself wishing I were in another profession. Each day seems exciting. When I come in each morning, I think I'm going to do certain things, but by nine o'clock the day may be completely devoted to an unanticipated event. I'm propelled by the changing pace, by the unusual and sometimes bizarre events that crop up on occasion. Like most of us, I cannot say that I always feel good about everything I experience on the job, but I've learned to keep a positive perspective on my work and on the decisions I have to make."

Leaders surveyed for our study go even farther in exemplifying the magnitude and range of qualities related to a positive attitude. Sherrill Ragans, associate vice-president for student affairs at Florida State University, names "enthusiasm and sheer physical, mental, and emotional energy." Murray DeArmond, director of student health services at the University of Arizona, mentions "a deep-seated optimism and enthusiasm for life and work." George Mills, dean of admissions at the University of Puget Sound, identifies optimism as important: "Many students become so focused on their objective that they do not have a balanced sense of the world and their relationship to it. Optimism and the ability to point out the other areas of association with the world are important in this regard."

Joshua Kaplan, director of the student health service at Bowling Green State University, evokes "the assumption that all is possible. I continue to be amazed at how often I can find solutions to apparently insoluble problems. I must add that this approach requires a desire to say yes. Those who enjoy demonstrating their power by vetoing suggestions and denying requests will not be helped by assuming that all is possible. But that assumption, combined with the desire to please all the people all the time, is very powerful."

John Koldus, vice-president for student services at Texas A & M University, says that he is "enthusiastic, positive, and optimistic" in his approach "to people, to life and its problems." Thomas Flynn, vice-president for student affairs at Monroe Community College, mentions "a positive attitude— an attitude which is contagious among student affairs staff. We believe whatever the job, we can get it done. If resources are not available, we will find them. If time is not available, we will become more efficient. It is amazing what can be accomplished when we know it can be." Kitty Arnold of Notre Dame stresses how important it is that this attitude come from the top of the organization: "In order to have an enthusiastic, energetic staff, one must also be enthusiastic and energetic. Managers cannot expect their employees to be more excited about their work than they themselves are."

"The perspective that nothing, or at least very little, is impossible" characterizes the approach of Jean Yerian, director of career planning and placement at Virginia Commonwealth University. "I've found that this attitude has been enormously significant for me. It allows me to try multiple approaches, rather than giving up at the first failure. It allows me to believe in people's potential, even when their present performance or circumstances are not promising. It encourages me to risk asking unanswerable questions, and to approach others with an air of expectancy and true collaboration. In short, it frees me from often defeating myself before I start."

Patrick Scheetz, assistant director of career development and placement services at Michigan State University, mentions a positive attitude in working with students, as well as with colleagues: "Although many negative vibrations hit us every day, it is necessary that we keep our heads and a positive orientation. Faced with a budget cut, we are responsible for using that negative and turning it into a positive, maybe even a budget increase for our area. When graduating students approach us with the news that their job campaigns have not been successful, it is our job to instill confidence in these individuals, so that they will continue looking and find entry-level opportunities commensurate with their qualifications. When university administrators question our analyses of job-market trends, it is our job to have plenty of statistics to prove our points, thus maintaining a positive orientation." For Scheetz, this positive, "can do" attitude assumes no room for negativism.

Passion

If excellence is to be achieved, passion must be cultivated, according to Peters and Austin (1985). This idea, first applied in business and industry, applies equally to student and academic services. Bennis (1989a) names vision as primary to leadership and passion as the second ingredient, "the underlying passion for the promises of life, combined with a very particular passion for a vocation, a profession, a course of action" (p. 40).

Armed with enjoyment of student services work and an optimistic outlook, institutional leaders develop passion. Jeanne Likins, former director of student life services at Ohio State University, eloquently discusses her commitment as passion: "Passion is belief, action, and care interwoven. The care includes love for what I do and a deep commitment to and concern for those with whom I work. Passion makes many things possible. It enables us to live with conviction and to

harbor visions of something better. It keeps our motivational
fires burning during times of disappointment, duress, and
stress. It gives us the energy to persist and to sprint the final
distance. It keeps alive a commitment to things greater than
the self."

The leaders surveyed for this study have a strong commitment to the profession, their institutions, their supervisors,
and the students they serve. This commitment is characterized
by a positive outlook and is evident in the satisfaction and
enjoyment they derive from their work, as well as in the conviction with which they fulfill their responsibilities.

Tenacity

Tenacity, for these leaders, involves a strong work ethic, efficiency, perseverance, and patience. There are also implications for personal credibility, related to follow-through on
work and to the ability to "deliver." Several studies (Stogdill,
1948; Bass, 1981; Bass and Stogdill, 1990; Yukl, 1981, 1989;
Gardner, 1990) have identified the personal qualities associated with tenacity. They include perseverance, diligence,
attention to detail, efficiency, persistence, and follow-through.
The leaders in this study call on all these characteristics, as
necessary, to do their work effectively.

Work Ethic

John Schuh, associate vice-president for student affairs at
Wichita State University, believes that hard work and efficiency are essential: "I believe that I make very good use of
my time and put in a full day's work nearly every day. What
this means is that I waste very little time and try to give
myself plenty of time to get things done, so that it is very rare
that I am under the gun with respect to meeting deadlines.
Some people have called me compulsive, in terms of my work.
I think that is quite accurate." Arthur Sandeen, vice-president
for student affairs at the University of Florida, mentions "a
willingness to put in long hours, organize well, and follow
up with staff members and students." For Schuh and San-

deen, organization is important; in addition to organization, however, the profession demands commitment beyond what is regarded as a "normal" work week.

Ray Franco, assistant vice-president for student affairs and director of residential services of the State University of New York at Cortland, emphasizes a strong work ethic but qualifies it by characterizing it as "a work ethic which always forces me to take my responsibilities seriously, without taking myself too seriously." "A willingness to work hard" has been helpful to Paul Moore, vice-president for student affairs at California State University, Chico. He says, "Working hard is more than long hours and twenty-four-hour commitment. It involves being a lifelong learner—that is, someone who is actively involved in life and in his or her life's work." Despite long work hours, the leaders surveyed for this study maintain a balanced perspective on their work and have the sense that they are learning and personally benefiting from it.

Perseverance

Another important element of tenacity is perseverance. Donald Gwinn, registrar at Northwestern University, places the importance of perseverance in the context of a longer-term career perspective: "There is a hierarchy of personal qualities necessary for success. When one is starting out, perseverance, attention to detail, and technical knowledge are qualities that are necessary to even get considered for a promotion. Once one gets into a leadership position, other qualities become more important." This statement implies that perseverance is a fundamental expectation in the administration of student services.

In discussing perseverance, Charles Nolan, dean of undergraduate admissions at Babson College, utilizes the imagery of running and sailing: "I believe that, as in a marathon, one needs to fix one's sights on the long-term goal and keep going, measuring success by seeing through the short-term objectives, which serve as benchmarks along the way. While perseverance—the ability to remain committed to a well-considered strategy—may sound terribly rigid, a good leader pursues his or her goals, not in linear fashion but more like the captain of a sailing vessel, tacking to the changing conditions. Reaching the ultimate goal, a good leader has persevered through the climatic vagaries, which constantly require shifting of the mainsail, jib, and rudder, taking advantage of the strength of the ship and crew." With this simile, Nolan gives us the sense that perseverance does not connote rigidity but instead implies the ability to adjust appropriately all along a course of action, so that the achievement of ultimate goals will be possible.

Charles Schroeder, vice-president for student services at Georgia Institute of Technology, believes that his tenacity has made a major difference in his career: "As one of my college professors stated in a recommendation, 'What Charles Schroeder doesn't have in native intelligence, he makes up for in perseverance.' My gifts clearly lie in organizational skills, high task/achievement orientation, ability to help staff members focus clearly on important issues and develop practical and reasonable ways to address them, and ability to communicate effectively with a wide range of constituents. Equally important, I place a premium on high expectations, for myself and others, and I attempt to communicate those expectations consistently throughout my division and the university." Schroeder's comments reflect the determination that characterizes tenacious people.

Perseverance also involves staying the course, regardless of obstacles. Freyda Lazarus, director of cooperative education at Montclair State College, says, "I have a vision of how this program should operate, and I am willing to stick it out during times of reduced budgets, changeover of key administrators, and internal political pressure."

Thomas Coyne, formerly of Western Michigan University, offers a wonderful analogy for staying the course. As he relates, "Years ago, I worked a summer as a third helper on the open hearths in the Youngstown Sheet and Tube Steel Mills in Indiana Harbor, Indiana. At the conclusion of the summer's work, a fellow third helper paid me a compliment that, over the years, has come to mean a great deal to me. He said, 'You did your share of the work.' In various jobs leading to this position, and during the past twenty years as vice-president for student services, I have come increasingly to feel that if I can continue to do *my* share of the work, I can live comfortably, not only with myself but also with the university, and its most important people—the students—will also benefit. It is not a profound philosophy, but it works." For Coyne, doing one's "share" represents the kind of perseverance so important in doing good work.

Patience

As an element of tenacity, patience characterizes the leaders surveyed for this study in some distinctive ways. Patience is not a passive trait. It actually involves appropriate timing and placement of responsibilities, engagement of others in a particular agenda, and the seeking of their true understanding.

William Edmonds, registrar and director emeritus of admissions at Gainesville College, feels that patience is a key to his success: "I have always seen my ability to listen patiently as the key factor. For example, people come to talk with me about admissions criteria. I have heard many stories—'Why I was suspended from whatever university'—hundreds of times over the past twenty-two years, but I make an effort to listen and understand, as though I were hearing it for the first time. The crux of the matter remains that it is this student's first time to tell the story, usually under great nervous stress, and confidence needs bolstering. 'Confession' is a great part of the cure, I believe, and certainly an important point in the turnaround process." Robert Bailey, registrar at the University of California, Berkeley, ties together "flexibility and patience. Every idea and plan has its time. Doing it tomorrow is better than not doing it at all. Also, some of these ideas need to be handed off or raised somewhere other than in your own office. It doesn't matter who gets the credit. The most important thing is to have a good idea implemented."

Gary Engelgau, executive director of admissions and records at Texas A & M University, mentions "just enough patience to attempt to understand why I am receiving the response I am from the person with whom I am talking. I do attempt to accept other people's positions as legitimate and worthy, and so if I don't agree, I have to at least understand why they are taking the positions they are. From there, we can often reach mutually satisfactory solutions." Obviously, careful attention and patience are essential ingredients of understanding.

Follow-Through

James Thomas, registrar at Colorado State University, identifies follow-through as an important attribute: "People need to depend upon you, or others in authority, to be inspired to follow or cooperate with them. If I say I will do something, I am compelled to do it, or at least get back to those to whom I am committed, in a timely fashion, with an explanation of any delay in my compliance."

An important aspect of follow-through is "attention to detail." Ron Weisinger, former assistant director of student life at the University of Rhode Island, says, "My primary responsibility was judicial affairs, which is a very technical area requiring expertise that most generalists don't have or need to have. I think I survived thirteen years in that role because I realized the need and enjoyed the challenge of being very precise, thorough, and deliberate. In judicial affairs, one is always dealing with a dispute or controversy of some sort. To be effective, I found it critical to avoid unnecessary distractions, such as technical challenges to due process. Careful attention to these details was my way of being effective and successful in that difficult arena. A keen sense of anticipation was helpful as well, in terms of preparing for the twists that always seemed to arise in serious cases." Effective performance requires the same attention to detail.

For Stuart Sharkey, vice-president for student affairs at the University of Delaware, follow-through is "the ability to be task oriented, to get the job done, to be counted on to meet deadlines, to effectively implement a proposal and deal with the tough issues." John Greisberger, director of the Office of International Students and Scholars at Ohio State University, puts the matter succinctly when he speaks of being "concerned with details." Being precise, attending to details, and meeting obligations are important elements of follow-through.

The leaders surveyed for this study assert the importance of tenacity as a characteristic of successful student services administrators. With a strong work ethic, perseverance, patience, and follow-through, leaders will have what Carmen Jordan-Cox, vice-president for student development at the University of San Francisco, calls tenacity: "the ability to focus on an agenda and to stick with it until the deed is done—the ability to deliver."

Reflections on Leaders' Thoughts

Integrity, commitment, and tenacity constitute the core attributes of institutional leaders. They serve as a wellspring from which leaders draw strength, keeping them focused and centered. These core attributes simultaneously offer a larger vision and guide day-to-day actions.

These attributes give shape and substance to the visions that these leaders have for their work. Listening to their words, one understands that their possession of these attributes allows them to model the best of what is possible for themselves, students, institutions, and the profession. These leaders assist and even propel institutions and people to be better. They seem to be "ahead of the curve" in identifying what is important and in taking hold of the issues and values that matter.

The attributes discussed in this chapter are visible to others on a daily basis, in countless individual decisions and interactions. Whether working with their superiors, with subordinates, with colleagues, or with students, whether on issues of recruitment, commuter services, or student government, these leaders are guided by integrity, commitment, and tenacity, and so the issues themselves, and the paths toward the resolution of problems, are clear.

CHAPTER THREE

Knowing How to Lead and How to Follow

Effective practitioners in student services understand how to be useful members of teams and organizations. Over twenty years ago, Tripp (1970a, 1970b) noted that the student affairs leader of the future would have to be both servant and leader. As the participants in this study talk about their varied roles, they make Tripp's prediction come alive. They demonstrate the special blend of qualities and skills that enables them to be both good leaders and good followers. In fact, Gardner (1990) observes that leading and following are overlapping and interactive and that most leaders are followers, in some context, while good followers are called on to perform leaderlike acts. Heller and Van Til (1982) also believe that leadership and followership are linked and can be understood only in tandem.

Collaborative Style

For the participants in this study, a collaborative style is essential, both for leading and for following. William Bryan, vice-chancellor for student affairs at the University of North Carolina, Wilmington, defines a collaborative relationship as "a partnership that can exist in an institution of higher education, as we are all, hopefully, concerned about the welfare and development of our campus clients—students." Lipman-Blumen (1989) describes this partnership as reflecting a connective style of leadership. Eugene Seeloff, assistant dean of career planning and placement in the School of Engineering and Applied Science at the University of Virginia, talks about how he establishes such a collaborative partnership: "Because we work in a continuously changing environment, I try to establish collaborative relationships and maintain an open dialogue with faculty, employees, and other career service professionals." Collaboration requires getting to know people, which necessitates an investment of time, according to Robert Oleson, vice-president for student affairs at Heidelberg College: "I spend a great deal of time on campus, probably three nights a week. I make sure that I have lunch or coffee at least twice a week with faculty. A number of them, obviously, are my personal friends. I believe strongly in the philosophy that it's a total community, that we are here for the students, and that my office is here to support the academic program of the institution." This understanding—that student services supports the academic mission—and this openness reflects a caring and responsible attitude and a willingness to collaborate and share power.

Bob Nielsen, chief of police at the University of Maryland, Baltimore County, assesses his own success by the degree to which he collaborates: "I determine how effective a job I'm doing by the openness and willingness with which people deal with me. I think my officers are usually quite open and honest with me because I always strive to listen and be fair. Equally important, I believe that all persons should be treated with respect, regardless of their rank or status. From chancellor to janitor, everyone deserves to be treated respectfully. This is hard for many administrators, who are accustomed to a rigid, military organization. If you show persons respect, they are likely to treat you respectfully in return."

Important elements of collaboration for these leaders are investing time, building relationships, and operating in an open, nonhierarchical manner. They treat all members of the community with respect and dignity. With so many reports suggesting that the lack of collaboration is the primary reason why higher education failed to address many pressing problems in the 1980s (Leatherman, 1991; Boyer, 1987; Gardner, 1990; Carnegie Foundation for the Advancement of Teaching, 1990), the messages of these leaders—about respect for others, and about collaboration—take on even greater meaning. From strong relationships and valuable collaborations, effective practitioners derive an understanding of their position in their organizations and institutions, as well as an understanding of the community's expectations of student services.

As participants share their views about being members of complex organizations in institutions of higher education, insights emerge about following and leading.

Following

The participants in this study clearly recognize their responsibilities to their supervisors. This recognition does not connote subservience, but it does reflect the participants' intention to serve the people to whom they report. The participants have said that they can best meet this goal by effectively managing their areas of responsibility and by using clear and confident communication.

Effective Management in the Institutional Culture

"Doing the right things" in a particular institutional culture has been stressed by several writers and entails developing individual operations in the light of institutional mission, philosophy, values, and style (Kuh, Schuh, Whitt, and Associates, 1991; Cameron, 1985; Dutton and Rickard, 1989). It requires a shared vision of the institution and its students (Kuh, Schuh, Whitt, and Associates, 1991).

Thomas Dutton, senior adviser to the chancellor and former vice-chancellor for student affairs at the University of California, Davis, says that what contributed most to his success as a leader was, first of all, "a basic understanding of institutional purpose, goals, priorities, and values. Without such an understanding, my leadership would have been ineffective." Raymond Heath, vice-president for student affairs at La Salle University, attributes much of his positive working relationship with his supervisor, the president, to the fact that "we approach issues confident that we agree on the mission of the university and the central role of the student affairs division." With clear understanding as a foundation, effective management in student affairs involves "organizing available human and fiscal resources to meet institutional and program goals in an efficient, effective, ethical, and fiscally responsible manner" (Barr, 1987, p. 9). Effective leaders organize services in such a way that they serve the overall goals of the institution.

Performance

The expected outcome of effective management is good performance. Kuh (1985) names "sticking to the knitting" (Peters and Waterman, 1982) as a primary characteristic of extraordinary student affairs organizations.

Effective practitioners feel that supervisors have a right to expect a high level of performance from their staff. David Butler, director of housing and residence life at the University of Delaware, answers the question of what supervisors expect: "The answer is simple: performance. The boss needs to know that clear goals are established and that at the end of the year significant progress has been made toward them." Stuart Sharkey, vice-president for student affairs at the University of Delaware, defines effective management as "the ability to be task oriented, to get the job done, to be counted on to meet deadlines, to effectively implement a proposal and deal with tough issues." Jimmy Epting, former vice-president for student development at North Greenville College, puts it succinctly:

"Results! Follow-through! Consistency!" Edward Jones, director of university housing at Southern Illinois University, Carbondale, characterizes this as "responsiveness." He says, "When my supervisor wants information or wants something done, I make those items my top priority."

Some participants in this study state outcome goals in very specific terms. George Mills, dean of admissions at the University of Puget Sound, says, "As dean of admissions, I report directly to the president of the university. The most important factor, as far as the president is concerned, is that the number of students necessary to meet the budget [be] enrolled and that the quality of the student body [be] such that faculty members may continue to expect of students the quality of work that they have expected in the past." Mills, Butler, Sharkey, Epting, and many other participants accept responsibility for the outcomes of their work.

When practitioners manage their areas effectively, there are many benefits for supervisors. Gerry Strumpf, director of orientation at the University of Maryland, College Park, says, "I believe that the greatest comfort for a secure administrator is that the operations that report to you are handled in an efficient manner, and that, as the chief student affairs administrator, you are not responsible for fighting their battles." Other participants agree that effective practitioners protect their supervisors from having to micromanage problems in their areas. David Ross, associate dean of student affairs at Central Connecticut State University, offers his perspective: "Supervisors that I have had appreciate someone who not only does not create problems but who also can take care of problems and keep them away from the supervisor." Thomas Dutton of the University of California, Davis, echoes this sentiment: "Over the past twenty-one years, under two chancellors, it has always been expected that I would cope with a wide range of complex student problems, with sensitivity and wisdom and with minimal difficulty for the institution. Chancellors like to feel that student issues are dealt with effectively at the vice-chancellor's level, so that problems do not end up on their desks." The leaders in this study have repeatedly affirmed that effective management entails running one's area so well that problems for one's supervisor are minimized. They also acknowledge that problems still arise even when management is effective.

Some participants have shared their perspectives on managing when difficulties arise. According to Stanley Levy, vice-chancellor for student affairs at the University of Illinois, "The best single example involves food service and residence halls. No matter what you try to do, you expect to find students complaining about dorm food. Our experience has been that we will get, at the level of our governing board or chief executive office, one or two complaints a year about residence hall food. We have been able to contain that problem by perhaps, in the eyes of some, bending over backwards and being good listeners to our students. Food service committees in the residence halls, advisory panels to the test kitchen, calorie counters, informational programs," and a variety of other specialized services are the outcomes of careful listening. Effective practitioners find creative ways to turn problems into opportunities and seek ways to listen to and include students in finding solutions. They also solve their own problems and do not expect their supervisors to solve them.

Image of Student Services

In considering the benefits to supervisors of effective management of their units, the participants were clear about how important effective management is to the positive image of student services on campus. James Braye, director of the Career Planning and Placement Center at the University of North Carolina, Wilmington, says, "The most important factor, from my supervisor's perspective, in whether I am doing an effective job is [whether] the office runs smoothly . . . and enjoys a good professional reputation among university professionals." Judith Mack, director of the counseling center at the University of California, Davis, comments, "I think the most important fact in my doing an effective job, from my supervisor's perspective, is twofold: the recognition from others on campus of the staff's good deeds, contributions to other programs, taking care of difficult students, and so on, and not having problems which bring negative attention to the unit or to an individual staff member."

Effective practitioners recognize that good management of their units reflects positively on the image and credibility of student services and of their supervisors. They provide support to their supervisors by effectively managing their own areas of responsibility. This entails achieving desired outcomes, solving problems effectively, and establishing a positive image for student services.

Clear Communication

The leaders surveyed for this study have developed close relationships with their supervisors, which can be characterized as open and loyal. James Grimm, director of housing at the University of Florida, observes, "I have been very fortunate in having served under four outstanding supervisors. All of these individuals have been very open and helpful and have had the welfare of the students as their first priority. My relationship with these supervisors was based on honesty, openness, and being up front." Clear and honest two-way communication is essential to the effective functioning of the leader-follower relationship (Gardner, 1990; Barr, Upcraft, and Associates, 1990).

Many leaders emphasize how important it is to keep supervisors informed about the issues that may come to their attention and about which they may be questioned. Alan Boyd, director of international student and faculty services at Ohio University, says, "I keep my supervisor informed when problems seem to be relevant to him. In fact, I think I am on the side of supplying him with more information than he needs." Eugene Ward, special assistant to the vice-president for student affairs at Southern Methodist University, agrees: "Good communication is essential to establishing trusting relationships with anyone. In the case of my supervisor, I try to keep him informed at all times, in order to minimize or eliminate surprises."

Margaret Barr, vice-chancellor for student affairs at Texas Christian University, reflects on how important it is to forewarn one's supervisor about issues that he or she may encounter: "I make it a point to let the chancellor know of any event or situation that he might hear of in casual conversation, through phone calls from interested parties, or the media. Examples include reported rapes, assaults, student activism, and so on. I do not like to be surprised, and neither does he. This enables him to be responsive if he is questioned, and he has the opportunity to seek additional information if he so desires." Tim Gallineau, vice-president for student development at Saint Bonaventure University, emphasizes how important it is to be completely candid with one's supervisor. He stresses the importance of "telling him what he needs to hear, not what he wants to hear." James Lyons, dean emeritus of student affairs at Stanford University, concurs: "I don't keep things from him—especially bad news, or issues that threaten difficulties in the future." Thus, an important element of being an effective follower is to communicate openly and fully with one's supervisor, even when the information one must present is negative.

In addition to preparing supervisors for potential questions and problems, it is important to communicate about other matters. Margaret Barr, vice-chancellor for student affairs at Texas Christian University, adds, "It's important to deal with specific events . . . and larger issues, such as racism. I try to specifically let him know what the issue is and how we are confronting it." Along similar lines, Thomas Myers, vice-president for student affairs at Eastern Kentucky University, explains, "I keep him informed on critical issues, advise him on how I plan to proceed, and sometimes ask for advice. I think he feels my support." Rosalind Andreas, vice-president for student affairs at the University of Vermont, says, "I believe it helps to be able to reflect an institutional view to address problems. I try always to do that with a supervisor, first to analyze a situation from an institutional perspective as well." This helps leaders be included in issues of institutional management. As William Paleen, director of residence

life at Cornell University, says, "Involvement in top-level management decisions has been enhanced by attempting to consistently and thoroughly communicate what we are doing and
how well it is being done. To some degree, this generates
awareness and credibility that you have something to add to
strategic institutional decision making." Effective followers
go beyond their own specific, assigned responsibilities. They
assume positions as institutional officers, helping their supervisors develop perspectives on broader issues.

The leaders surveyed for this study also discuss how
one presents problems or issues to supervisors. John Bannister, director of financial aid at the University of South Carolina, has some sound advice: "You should preface your
opinion with a comment like, 'This is my recommendation,
but here are some alternatives you may wish to consider.'
Giving one's supervisor the most complete information, as
well as alternatives and your preferred option, is obviously
important." The participants feel confident that the information they provide is valued by their supervisors and that their
advice will be heard and heeded. This is a contemporary inter-
pretation of Simmel's (1950) notion that followers have as
much influence on leaders as leaders have on them.

Knowing when to communicate is also important. Kenneth Burda, formerly vice-chancellor for student affairs, currently vice-president for institutional advancement, at the
State University of New York at New Paltz, says, "I believe
that timing is a critical skill that all successful managers must
have. It is a very difficult skill to teach but, when mastered, it
becomes an important component of success. Timing is critical in dealing with supervisors, as well as with subordinates.
Asking the right question at the wrong time, or giving appropriate directions at the wrong time, can lead to disaster and
can mask the reasons why the disaster occurred. Very often, it
is not the material involved, but the process of delivery. I
have heard this skill referred to as *seasoning,* which means to
allow an important decision to be looked at carefully and a
strategy for implementation to be developed."

The participants have noted the importance of voicing

an honest opinion, being prepared to disagree, and knowing that one has a responsibility to support a supervisor's final decision. Gardner (1990) says that dissent is a natural part of effective communication, and some healthy organizations rely on disagreement as a facet of accurate feedback (Birnbaum, 1988). The leaders surveyed for this study agree. Dorothy Anderson, dean of students at Susquehanna University, advises staff members to "choose wisely about whether to argue, being sure you understand the facts before you take a position." Participants emphasize the importance of voicing disagreement but then being willing to be a team player after a decision is reached. About discussing work with the president, James Lyons of Stanford says, "There are a few times when we may disagree on some matters. When that happens, I disagree—either in my periodic one-on-one meetings with him or in the cabinet or other forums. That disagreement does not find its way back into public forums, partly because I know that he will hold back on an issue if I have strong feelings about it." Effective followers are honest about disagreements but act as team players when it is important for institutional leaders to present a united front.

Participants use a variety of methods of communication. Samuel Sadler, vice-president for student affairs at the College of William and Mary, schedules regular meetings with the president and informs him in advance of the agenda: "In the time we have together, I focus on a few important topics, rather than trying to cover a wide range of items." James Lyons of Stanford affirms the importance of regular meetings with one's supervisor: "I make use of the forums he established in order to communicate. In my case, this is at least two weekly meetings." Thomas Coyne, former vice-president for student services at Western Michigan University, agrees: "I have weekly one-on-one meetings, to which I bring an agenda and information that is thought out in advance and concise." Effective leaders emphasize the importance of regular meetings with supervisors and note the importance of having a clear agenda in advance.

Where information exchange is concerned, some leaders

broaden the definition of *supervisor* to include other institutional leaders. Thomas Dutton, senior adviser to the chancellor at the University of California, Davis, explains, "I meet with the chancellor and vice-chancellor and deans twice a week, and this provides the opportunity to interact with key administrative officers. I take advantage of these meetings to present campus issues and to seek counsel." Again, the collaborative style of participants emerges. They regularly inform their colleagues and supervisors. They seek input, and they adapt and act on the basis of this input.

There are other methods besides meetings that the participants employ to communicate. They emphasize respecting the schedules and demands of their supervisors. Robert Oleson, vice-president for student affairs at Heidelberg College, notes, "My main supervisor is the president of the institution. The time spent with him is usually over the phone or in short memos back and forth." Effective following entails sensitivity to one's supervisor's schedule and needs and lets those serve as guides to type and frequency of communication.

Effective leaders also note that there is something to be gained in occasionally deviating from routine types of communication. John Bannister, director of financial aid at the University of South Carolina, suggests an innovative approach to communication: "At least once a year, go to your boss and ask, 'What do we do that hampers you and makes your job difficult?'" This comment reflects the view that effective leaders continually strive to improve the support they give their supervisors.

The participants in this study recommend frequent and regular meetings with supervisors, the use of written memos when appropriate, and yearly or other long-term assessments of ways to improve support of supervisors.

Leading

The participants in this study have a variety of leadership styles and a limitless number of creative approaches to leadership. Amid all the differences, some common elements emerge. Leaders espouse values that provide a frame of reference. They have visions that embody their values, and they develop plans to actualize their visions.

Values

The importance of value-driven leadership has been noted in the literature. Fink (1988) calls on leaders to articulate their core values and to ensure that their behavior is consistent with them. Others (Peters and Waterman, 1982) go even farther, saying that effective leaders unite the social forces in an organization to shape and guide values. The leaders surveyed for this study believe in the importance of value-driven leadership, and they articulate the values that guide them. Three values emerge as primary: fundamental belief in the worth, dignity, and developmental potential of students; strong commitment to racial, cultural, and ethnic diversity; and belief in the positive power of a constructive environment.

Worth, Dignity, and Developmental Potential

For the leaders surveyed for this study, the most important value is the belief in all students' worth, dignity, and developmental potential. Alfred Matthews, vice-chancellor for student life at East Carolina University, characterizes this as the belief that "individuals, rather than knowledge, are the center of the learning process." He elaborates by emphasizing that "each student is unique and deserving of recognition of his or her worth and dignity."

The importance of students is emphasized by many leaders. William Butler, vice-president for student affairs at the University of Miami, affirms this value: "Students are central to the mission in higher education." This centrality is evident in a statement of the philosophy of the housing program at the University of Delaware, where David Butler is director of housing and residence life. The statement says, "The primary focus of the office of residence life is student development." Leaders feel that students and their development should be valued above all else.

　　　Some leaders emphasize how important it is to work for an institution that values students. Joan Claar, dean of students at DePauw University, says, "It is important to me that students are seen and treated as partners in the educational enterprise, and not simply as customers who must be tolerated and mollified."

Racial, Cultural, and Ethnic Diversity

Leaders surveyed for this study value diversity highly. Linda Kuk, vice-president for student affairs of the State University of New York, College at Cortland, says, "Campus diversity is a major goal of our profession and one that I have been personally committed to for my entire professional career." Alice Manicur, vice-president for student and educational services at Frostburg State University, also expresses this spirit: "I am committed to do whatever I can to make the campus environment a place where we can all function effectively, recognizing our differences and appreciating our cultural heritages."

　　　Larry Moneta, associate vice provost for university life, University of Pennsylvania, talks about how one reflects these values in action: "I feel as if I respond to diversity on several levels. Perhaps the most important way in which I pay attention to differences among students is by carrying acknowledgment of difference as a filter through which all I do passes. I believe that to be a multicultural administrator or educator one has to consider the implications of every decision and every act on the different cultures, religions, sexual orientations, classes, and so on, which make up our campus communities. Much as any good administrator automatically considers the financial implications of any decision, an effective leader must be equally attentive to the implications of decisions for the different schedules, dietary needs, and other culturally unique aspects of our constituencies. But that's not enough. The response to diversity must also include deliberate efforts to accomplish several objectives. The unique needs of different communities must be supported through services, programs, and activities which address those needs. All students must be exposed to difference through interventions which build coalitions and enable a celebration of what makes us all different from one another. Activities must be sponsored to address biases and prejudice and to counter the destructive effects of racism, sexism, homophobia, antisemitism, and all other forms of oppression." Moneta expresses the essential orientation of Schön's "reflective practitioner" (1987).

Others stress the importance of modeling. Sherrill Ragans, associate vice-president for student affairs at Florida State University, says, "On our campus, modeling egalitarian and nonprejudicial behavior is the best way to improve race relations. Letting students and staff members see that you treat all people at all levels of the hierarchy with dignity and respect is crucial." This entails personal involvement. Alice Manicur of Frostburg State University says, "I like to give my personal support by attending events sponsored by minority students, by encouraging them to become involved in student organizations, and by providing role models on the staff, both student and professional members. We can communicate our position by initiating and supporting actions to alleviate all forms of discrimination on the campus."

Apart from drawing clear limits, not tolerating bigotry, and modeling egalitarian behavior, leaders talk about extending this value beyond themselves. Larry Moneta, speaking of his previous position as associate director for residential education at the University of Massachusetts, Amherst, recalls, "I was fortunate to have a fairly large staff of color and to be working in an environment which actively celebrated difference, combatted oppression, and cherished diversity. This principle embraced every facet of our operation."

Constructive Environment

A third value emphasized by leaders in this study relates to creating a constructive and positive community environment for students. William Butler of the University of Miami values "creating a quality environment that fosters students' growth and development." Alfred Matthews of East Carolina University describes this as "a caring university with a healthful environment." One essential aspect of a constructive environment is its developmental and healthy nature. Matthews calls attention to another important element: "the management of the interfaces between services and programs." Other elements of a constructive community environment are its caring, its developmental focus, and its coherence.

Vision

According to Caple and Newton (1991), effective leaders articulate their values and, in acting on them, find a source of empowerment. This process is evident for effective leaders in student services. They discuss their strongly held values and, empowered by their strong convictions, have clear visions of the future of their organizations or systems. Hickman and Silva (1984) define *vision* as "a mental journey from the known to the unknown, creating a future from a montage of facts, hopes, dreams, dangers, and opportunities" (p. 15). Bennis (1989a) says that vision is a basic ingredient of leadership. Kouzes and Posner (1987) describe "inspiring a shared vision" as a process that leaders use to bring about extraordinary accomplishments in their organizations. Komives (1991), in her study of gender differences, leadership, and achieving styles, affirms the importance of inspiring and empowering staff. The participants in this study speak eloquently of how important it is to have vision. This involves developing a mental image of a possible and desirable state for an organization, understanding how this vision fits in with the larger vision for the institution, and motivating others to embrace that vision (Bensimon, Neuman, and Birnbaum, 1989).

James Osteen, director of the Stamp Student Union at the University of Maryland, College Park, says, "I try to present a vision of what could be possible for our organization. This involves, first, stating goals that are beyond our current operating level and, second, describing scenarios of what our organization would be like if we were to accomplish these goals." William Klepper, dean of student life at Trenton

State College, also emphasizes the importance of vision: "I prove leadership in my position by envisioning new directions, programs, and goals for the division while maintaining the quality of our existing services to students and to the college community. Thomas Dutton, of the University of California, Davis, characterizes this as a "matter of driving and trying to fix the automobile simultaneously." Participants effectively manage their areas, but, as leaders, they also have clear ideas for improvement of their areas or organizations.

Murray DeArmond, director of the student health service at the University of Arizona, says that, for him, "a sense of vision for the ideal campus health unit has been a powerful motivation. I've always been interested in the larger questions, in spite of having been trained in a reductionist profession. How student health services are related to student affairs, to the student affairs profession, to student development theory, and to overall institutional goals have been questions of continuing interest to me." Gardner (1990) describes this kind of thinking as conceptualizing the "visible future," whereby leaders employ long-term thinking to help organization members ascertain how the system fits into a larger context and envision what is possible.

In defining *vision*, participants note that there is risk. Eugene Seeloff, assistant dean in the School of Engineering and Applied Science at the University of Virginia, defines the vision and the risk as "trying to visualize or conceptualize what should be (and encouraging others to do the same) and working toward that vision; challenging old ways of doing things, and changing to new ways if they are better—by soliciting input and ideas on many issues, and by trying to do the right things in the right ways—most of the time! By being willing to risk doing something [that is] less than perfect, we can more often enjoy the passion of doing it right."

Action

The indisputable outcome of leadership is action. Leadership, according to Burns (1978), means inducing followers to act and attain the goals that represent the values and motivations, wants and needs, and aspirations and expectations of leaders and followers alike. DePree (1989) makes an essential connection between vision and action: "Momentum comes from a clear vision of what the corporation ought to be, from a well-thought-out strategy to achieve that vision, and from carefully conceived and communicated directions and plans which enable everyone to participate and be publicly accountable in achieving those plans" (p. 15).

An important element of implementing and operationalizing vision is enlisting staff members. Leaders have the challenge of using their vision to motivate others and provide a strong enough stimulus for change to overcome inertia (Fink, 1988). This involves drawing others into the vision.

Laurence Smith, vice-president for university marketing and student affairs at Eastern Michigan University, says, "A leader is one who can inspire others to buy into his vision. The vision can be created by the leader, borrowed, adopted, or adapted. It is the process of inspiring others to buy into it and stick with it that is the key ingredient of leadership. I believe that this is the particular skill which has contributed most to my success." Marvin Herrington, chief of police at Stanford University, comments, "The greatest obstacle to success is to discover that your clear vision of how to develop a superior service is either misunderstood or ignored by the people who must make it work—your staff." Phyllis Mable, vice-president for student affairs at Longwood College, says, "The vision must fit the needs, even dreams, of the constituencies."

Jean Yerian, director of career planning and placement at Virginia Commonwealth University, elaborates on this notion: "Leadership is a concept that challenges me daily to apply my creative energy to task and relationships. When I am an effective leader, I think it is often from my vision and willingness to involve others in building homes for their dreams. At my best, I honor the best in others and touch something in them that is unique and special, in service of a shared goal." DePree (1989) also stresses this point, noting that belief in the potential of people is essential to true participative management. He emphasizes the importance of respecting the gifts that people bring to organizations. Larry Moneta, associate vice-provost for university life of the University of Pennsylvania, also discusses the importance of touching what is important to others: "I depend heavily on my skill to bring out the best in others. I ask that my staff, the students with whom I work, and my colleagues work with high standards, and I prod, nudge, prompt, and occasionally kick, as necessary, to have them meet and exceed these standards." Maccoby (1976) asserts that leaders must bring out the best in people, and he defines that as "constructive ideals of a social character, the values that express [the] most positive traits" (p. 16).

Effective leaders seem to be able to tap into shared values and enlist others in accomplishing goals. As Jean Yerian of Virginia Commonwealth University says, "Leading well is the most difficult thing I have ever done, and the results are ever mixed. I find it hard to sustain the attentiveness, individuality, and focus needed to be a good leader. I often falter and fall back to more activity and direction. But even the few moments have such power and productivity that they enrich my life and keep me at this constant quest."

Enlisting others in embracing one's vision entails encouraging alternative opinions, ideas, and ways of doing things. Effective leaders are secure enough to risk sharing their own beliefs and ideas and to risk conflict and criticism (Fink, 1988). Charles Nolan, dean of undergraduate admissions at Babson College, notes that we can do that "simply by establishing an organizational culture which questions the conventional wisdom and status quo of our own work and that of our colleagues, both on and off campus." Rob Rouzer, director of Wilson Commons/Student Activities at the University of Rochester, values different opinions: "Leaders need to be able to listen to their followers and then create a united program out of the separate expressions." Thus, we find effective leaders valuing people who will question, challenge, change, redefine, and improve their own vision.

As leaders develop action plans and motivate staff members to embrace their visions, they are careful to pace themselves. Rosalind Andreas, discussing the changes she implemented in her previous position at the University of Arizona, recalls, "The challenge was how to inspire vision, without moving so rapidly that people did not feel a part of the process but only assaulted and threatened by it." Obviously, the process of developing plans is important, and leaders emphasize having a plan or a model. William Klepper of Trenton State College illustrates: "The approach that I use to motivate staff members has been to sell a conceptual model on which they can base their actions. Conceptual models allow us to rise above our individual desires, to those of the organization and the clientele we serve." Klepper also feels that conceptual models are defined "by corresponding goals and objectives." Sylvia Lujan, associate dean of the College of Arts and Sciences and director of the Learning Assistance Center at the University of Texas, Pan American, says that, as a result of clearly spelling out goals and objectives, she and her staff "know what our purpose is and how we fit into the institution's mission."

Unit goals and objectives should fit into the larger missions of student affairs and the institution. Wilbur Venerable, former director of admissions and records at Illinois State University, explains, "A good leader makes clear to all staff members how important their assignments are and how they are related to the overall mission of the office."

A conceptual model with clear goals and objectives enables people to get a sense of forward movement. Michael Hoctor, director of housing and residential life at San Diego State University, says, "Having adopted and implemented this management model in our department several years ago, we know where we are going, produce an enormous amount of work, and feel happy to be coming to work every day." Jimmy Epting of North Greenville College also mentions the importance of involving others in planning. For Epting, "involving all staff members in establishing goals and objectives, considering relevant alternatives, planning and implementing activ-

ities, and accepting responsibility for outcomes" are the core
of effective leadership. Carl Anderson, vice-president emeritus
for student affairs at Howard University, also believes in motivating staff members in this process: "We establish our goals
and objectives as a unit, so that we are all committed to what
we are going to do." David Hansen, associate dean for student
development at the University of Nevada, Reno, states this
principle well: "People tend to support what they help create."

In developing action plans, leaders emphasize the
necessity of staying on course. Sara Boatman, former director
of campus activities and programs at the University of
Nebraska, Lincoln, now chair of the department of communications and theatre arts at Nebraska Wesleyan University,
says that conventional planning, coupled with creative ideas,
can sometimes entice people to stretch in ways that contribute
to exhaustion and burnout. She stresses the importance of
strategic planning. Such planning, she recalls, "guided our
team's life. We were still enthusiastic and creative, but we
had a specific set of criteria against which to measure new
ideas and requests. . . . Strategic planning had become much
more than a buzzword for our team. It had become an essential tool for long-term organizational health and effectiveness.
It provided us a way to keep our talents and enthusiasm
focused and to use them in meaningful and realistic ways."
Priest, Alphenaar, and Boer (1980) state that long-range planning does not necessarily provide solutions but does help
administrators make rational choices among the available
alternatives.

As leaders realize their value-based visions, they incorporate the ideas and visions of others. They employ conceptual
models, establish clear goals and objectives, and continually
and carefully assess and evaluate their progress in order to stay
on course.

Reflections on Leaders' Thoughts

The leaders surveyed for this study employ a collaborative
style of interaction with faculty members, students, and the

staff members in their units. They would agree with Miller and Prince (1976) that collaboration is essential to the success of student development programs. With collaboration as a foundation, leaders discuss other characteristics that they believe to be essential to effective leading and following.

One essential element is an understanding of the interdependence of leadership and followership. Effective leaders are effective followers. The keys to effective following include managing one's area effectively, performing effectively in one's position, establishing clear and open lines of communication with one's supervisors, and cultivating a positive image for student services. The keys to effective leading include value-driven leadership, clear values, a vision for improvement, and actualization of those agendas.

As leaders talk about leading and following, the fluidity of their roles is apparent. The characteristics of each role aid in the effective execution of both. This idea supports Gardner's notion (1990) that most leaders are called on to be followers in some settings, and that followers are sometimes called on to perform leaderlike tasks. The leaders surveyed for this study are accomplished in both dimensions.

The importance of a collaborative, nonhierarchial style is mentioned by many leaders. This finding may stem in part from the peculiar niche of student affairs in higher education. To accomplish their ends, student affairs professionals must rely on others in academic and administrative affairs. For example, efforts to respond to students' concerns may involve academic departments for content and campus police for security. The need to reach out to diverse campus personnel may also require a collaborative style.

The collaborative style may be characteristic of a profession that is value driven. *The Student Personnel Point of View* (American Council on Education, 1937, 1949) and *A Perspective on Student Affairs* (National Association of Student Personnel Administrators, 1987) clearly state that viewing students holistically is a key to this kind of work. With this understanding, and with a developmental theory base and the thrust that it implies, the importance of joining with others across disciplines and functions to accomplish these ends is an idea that follows logically. This may be one of the qualities that makes the student affairs profession unique.

With a collaborative style as an umbrella, effective leaders are also good followers. They integrate their roles with a style that is nonhierarchical and inclusive and with a clear end in mind—the creation of integrative, developmental environments for students.

CHAPTER FOUR

Creating
a Supportive
Campus Environment

$\mathbf{E}$ffective leaders in student ser-
vices practice their profession in institutions that vary in size,
structure, governance, affiliations, fiscal support, and student
population. Despite this diversity, many leaders see the same
institutional characteristics as having contributed the most to
their success. The five mentioned most frequently are clarity
of institutional mission, congruence of institutional values,
promotion of an ethical environment, inclusion of student
services in institutional decision making, and full participation of student services in the budgetary process.

Institutional Mission

The leaders surveyed for this study encourage student affairs
practitioners to be certain they understand the missions of
their institutions. Indeed, a clear and distinctive institutional
mission is cited as a condition necessary for success in student
affairs work (Barr, Upcraft, and Associates, 1990). John Schuh,

associate vice-president for student affairs at Wichita State University, states, "I think I understand the mission of our institution very well and have tailored our new initiatives to be consistent with our mission. Our brightest successes have been mission driven. I would urge anyone considering a move to a new institution to study the mission statement. It will reveal a great deal about an institution."

Others also believe that a good mission statement is as important to a college or university as good management is, and that this mission statement should guide management (Martin, 1985). In discussing the missions of their institutions, many leaders have made it clear that their institutions are focused. For William Klepper, dean of student life at Trenton State College, the institution's vision statement has provided the framework for success: "The statement focuses on four values—service, excellence, diversity, and high expectations." Phyllis Mable, vice-president for student affairs at Longwood College, says, "My institution is committed to the total education of each student, and this commitment is reflected in an effort to provide an atmosphere supportive of individual development."

The student-centered approach is also noted by Frank Julian, former vice-president for student development at Murray State University. He relates that the primary characteristics enabling his success are "the student-centered mission of the institution and our constant pounding home of that point. If we are to put students first, then what happens to them inside and outside the classroom becomes the institution's top priority and ensures a supportive atmosphere for the student development staff." Nancy Wood, former director of tutorial services at the University of Texas, Arlington, talks about maintaining student-centered values by "reminding people of students' best interests—their right to learn without interruption."

Some leaders at land-grant institutions feel that those institutions' particular missions reflect the student-centered, caring ethic. James Quann, registrar and director of student information systems at the University of California, Santa

Cruz, names "the land-grant philosophy of outreach and helping others" as also having been extremely important at his former institution, Washington State University. Discussing the land-grant mission, Thomas Goodale, vice-president for student affairs at Virginia Polytechnic Institute and State University, says, "At Virginia Tech, we have students who live by the work-and-play ethic. They are able academically, but they also like to have fun. They are very goal oriented, in keeping with the land-grant tradition; the work ethic is very solid here. Virginia Tech has long been a center of caring for students, and I have had the good fortune to fall into that fine tradition."

Barr, Upcraft, and Associates (1990) share this perspective, noting the importance to student affairs work of a clear and definitive philosophy that guides the institution's relationship with students. The leaders surveyed for this study would concur. They understand the missions of their institutions and the values that those missions represent, and they feel particularly supported when these missions reflect a strong concern for student development.

Institutional Values

In a coherent organization, the mission reflects the values of the institution, and the actions of institutional leaders should also reflect these values (Miller, Winston, and Associates, 1991). Gardner (1990) believes that we should judge leaders within the framework of their values. The leaders surveyed for this study have a strong sense of institutional values, as well as an emotional commitment to those shared values. Margaret Barr, vice-chancellor for student affairs at Texas Christian University, says, "This is a value-driven institution, and we make no apologies for it. Care of persons is an important dimension of institutional culture and is carefully modeled by the chief executive officer. Further, a spirit of ecumenism and nondiscrimination pervades the campus environment." Charles Schroeder, vice-president for student services at the Georgia Institute of Technology, also views a value-centered institution as an asset. He made this statement at the time our study took place, when he was employed by Saint Louis University: "[The] institution is very value centered. Fortunately, the values of the institution are quite congruent with my personal and professional values. In particular, I find [the] fundamental mission—educating men and women for others—to reflect my concern for justice and fairness."

Congruence of personal and institutional values is also important to other participants in this study. Joan Claar, dean of students at DePauw University, says, "In considering new positions, the values of the institution and the congruence of those values with my personal values have been major considerations for me. Those values do *not* involve the age of students, the ability of students, the location of the institution, or the size or type of institution. They *do* involve the institution's 'attitude' toward students and their educational experience, and the way students are treated." This perspective reflects a belief also found in Miller, Winston, and Associates (1991): that real values are demonstrated in day-to-day experience on college campuses.

Other leaders share Claar's idea that being student centered is an important institutional value. Thomas Dutton, former vice-chancellor for student affairs at the University of California, Davis, and now senior adviser to the chancellor, reflects: "How our campus has viewed students and their learning . . . definitely enhanced my effectiveness as vice-chancellor for student affairs over . . . twenty-one years. The campus has always been student oriented, concerned about students' developmental needs, and committed to offering the best possible instruction and student affairs services." This comment reflects a view shared by Canon (1989), who asserts that student services professionals, more than any other group in higher education, attend to students' human needs and are concerned about individual differences.

David Butler, director of housing and residence life at the University of Delaware, talks about how an individual department can give credence to this notion: "The Office of

Housing and Residence Life, with considerable employee input, established a statement of department values. One of these, integrity, focuses on the need to be straightforward and honest in all of our transactions with students and each other." Butler's example shows how a student affairs unit can develop behavioral standards that reflect values.

Gary Althen, foreign student adviser at the University of Iowa, clearly identifies the value orientation of his campus: "There is a cultural, or traditional, concern on this campus with human rights, fairness, and equality. The University of Iowa takes pride in the fact that it was the first state university to admit female students. It seems that this general concern with fairness and equality generalizes to other aspects of campus life." Such values as justice, civility, fairness, and decency are based on beliefs about human nature and about what brings cohesiveness to a college campus (Martin, 1985). When these values become entrenched in day-to-day life, as Althen describes, they become for all community members invisible "threads in the fabric of their daily lives" (Kuh, Schuh, Whitt, and Associates, 1991).

Gardner (1990) describes the leader's role as one of "affirming values." Some astute observers of organizations even assert that the management of institutional values is the primary task of leaders (Peters and Waterman, 1982). The leaders surveyed for this study reflect this idea as they talk with pride about the values of their institutions. They seem to embrace these values as their own and find a focus in them for their work.

Commitment to Ethics

With our history and philosophical commitments, leaders in the profession must be advocates of individual dignity and worth, fairness, equity, and an ethical environment of the highest possible quality (Canon, 1989). In their discussions of institutional values, the commitment to an ethical climate emerges as a primary concern of effective leaders. They cogently discuss the importance of an ethical environment and the ways in which individual staff members can maintain it.

Some leaders surveyed for this study talk about the importance of guidelines, rules, and contracts. William Klepper of Trenton State College says, "Ethics never operate in a vacuum. By definition, ethical behavior dictates that one makes choices. A campus climate can contribute to ethical choices if it has at its core a clear statement of principles. In the past, I have found an efficient way to state these principles has been in the form of a social contract. I am defining a social contract in the spirit of Rousseau and the current thinking of Kohlberg. The statement of principles as a social contract requires that members of the community collectively arrive at the behavioral expectations they hold for one another." Klepper goes on to talk about how this ideal is put into practice: "Each year, in our professional staff and student groups, we develop statements of behavioral expectations, which are then held in common and used as a guide for individual behavior. This guide then becomes a standard against which to make judgments and choices. In the absence of this guide, the individual's wants, versus a collective need, would take priority. With the social contract, group values become the guide for principled behavior, thus creating an ethical campus climate."

James Rauker, vice-president for student affairs at Worcester State College, also talks about the importance of guidelines: "Clear and fair guidelines seem to be the most helpful. This provides everyone the opportunity to view a particular ethical issue in terms of what is and is not appropriate behavior. Anything outside of the guidelines would generally be interpreted as being beyond what one should be doing ethically. In my experience, the lack of clear guidelines and policies often invites people to make inappropriate decisions."

Winston Shindell, director of Indiana Memorial Union at Indiana University, agrees: "The campus must adopt an overall philosophy which incorporates a code of ethics. This code must be followed and strongly enforced at the highest levels of administration and faculty. We are all role models, and our actions must constantly reinforce what we state to be our beliefs. When violations of the code occur, action must be swift, fair, and consistent."

The code of conduct is one way of achieving clarity about expectations. Chris Ogle, associate dean of students and director of housing at Ripon College, believes that "the most important ingredient is to clearly outline expectations."

Richard Stimpson, assistant vice-president for student affairs at the University of Maryland, College Park, says, "I have found that well-articulated statements, which express the values we expect members of our community to uphold, help create an ethical climate on campus. Whether delivered during orientation, expressed at campus workshops or convocations, or presented in handbooks or manuals, these expressions set and reinforce an ethical standard, which helps shape individual decisions and actions on a daily basis." Stimpson feels, however, that the existence of guidelines alone is not enough: "I have found that open discussion regarding the best course of action, when a complex, value-laden decision needs to be made, helps maintain an ethical climate. As is frequently the case, the correct ethical decision is often not clear-cut and obvious. The opportunity to openly discuss different perspectives encourages decisions which are thoughtfully arrived at and consistent with community values."

Another leader talks about "understandings," rather than guidelines or rules; like Stimpson, Alan Boyd, director of international student and faculty services at Ohio University, emphasizes the importance of communication: "The whole campus is committed to an ethical climate, at least in theory. I help to maintain it by communicating with people and contributing my point of view, which I hope is fundamentally ethical. We also conduct workshops for staff and others, in which ethical questions are raised. In the process, I hope to achieve an understanding that we are all fallible people . . . and we need to recognize that. Then we can work on hearing others' points of view and try to achieve a more just campus. For, in the end, ethics is not a set of rules, but rather the achievement of justice in the midst of rights and wrongs, most of which are not very clear in this world of relativity." Boyd and Stimpson would agree that there is ambiguity in ethical decision making, and that full and open discussion can assist in the process.

Hearing different points of view and raising questions are important elements of an ethical environment. The late Wayne Carlisle, who was director of placement and career services at Wichita State University, advised practitioners to "constantly ask questions of others about how decisions, policies, and programs will affect people." David Taylor, vice-president for student affairs at Boise State University, says, "By raising questions with the president, vice-presidents, deans, department heads, and so on, about the rightness of any university action, a general ethical climate can be developed." Judith Chambers, vice-president for student life at the University of the Pacific, comments, "Perhaps the best [way to] approach [ethical issues] is by raising questions that need to be addressed and by making sure others do so as well." Larry Moneta, associate vice-provost for university life at the University of Pennsylvania, agrees: "I insist that my department be open to challenges, questions, and reviews. Decisions are shared, not hoarded; therefore, actions are always subject to accountability and justification. An ethical climate, to me, is one in which someone can choose to act, or not act, on personal or organizational convictions, [but] only if those convictions can be expressed openly, without fear of reprisal."

Institutional leaders contribute mightily to the development of an ethical climate. Gary Althen, foreign student adviser at the University of Iowa, says, "An important contribution to high technical standards is the behavior and statements of the university's highest-level administrators." He elaborates in discussing his own institution: "I believe the leadership here has, for a long time, consciously tried to establish and maintain an atmosphere in which high ethical standards are expected. The leaders themselves have been people of high standards, and they have frequently established standards which, implicitly or explicitly, also called on others to maintain high standards. They have made themselves available to discuss ethical issues with staff or faculty members who have such issues troubling them. I myself have been in meetings where a difficult situation was discussed, and the representative of the administration would ask, 'What's the right thing to do here?' " Leaders like Althen and the others cited here take pride in the existence of an ethical campus environment.

The leaders surveyed for this study emphasize that responsibility for an ethical environment extends beyond the president and his or her board of directors. Jeanne Likins, former director of student life services at Ohio State University, says, "Whatever one's position, this is something that can be done in the course of one's daily life. In our work with students, we should strive to model ethical behavior, and we should engage students in discussions about ethics. As advocates for students, we should strive to ensure that our colleagues are cognizant of the ethical dimensions of institutional policies and actions and the ethical environment which results from these." Brown (1985) also emphasizes the importance of modeling ethical behavior and being a "moral conscience" for the campus.

Leaders emphasize that ethical dilemmas are not esoteric issues but part of everyday life. Barbara Jacoby, director of the Office of Commuter Affairs at the University of Maryland, College Park, says, "In my office, we talk about 'EDs' [ethical dilemmas]. In staff meetings, I regularly describe those that I face or have faced. For resolved dilemmas, I often talk about what I decided, and why. For current issues, I often describe the situation and request suggestions. I believe that, all too often, we assume that we share an understanding of ethics, but that we really do not. Open discussion of the choices we make helps establish ethical standards."

The leaders surveyed for this study share a commitment to an ethical environment. Some emphasize the importance of rules and guidelines; others stress the more flexible notion of "understandings." No matter what their terminology, all agree that at the heart of an ethical environment is a commitment to principles. This commitment begins with the president and extends to all community members and to all types of day-to-day actions.

Inclusion in Institutional Decision Making

The leaders surveyed for this study are conscious of the roles they can play and the contributions they can make to institutional decision making. Participation in shared leadership is an important element of the development of community (Gardner, 1990). Leaders recognize competence in their functional areas as important to contributing at the institutional level, but they also note the importance of understanding how the various facets of the institution work, as well as the importance of an investment in the success of the overall institutional enterprise.

To be included, leaders must demonstrate that they are competent managers. Ruth Jass, former director of institutional research and registrar at Bradley University, says, "Earned respect makes a manager's opinion count. A long record of being prepared, of having accurate data and information, of making good decisions, will build confidence in the manager's ability to participate, and patent honesty will build trust among academic colleagues. When solid bridges are built between the manager and the faculty, the perspective of that manager will be sought out and valued as decisions are made." Jean Yerian, director of career planning and placement at Virginia Commonwealth University, agrees: "Decisions are shared on the basis of trust built through solid track records. I have believed for a long time in contributing all I can of what talents I have and in risking reasonable failure at some tasks wanted by none. I also know that trust comes from addressing issues through initiative. I want the support of others, and I try to establish appropriate competence with those above in the organization."

Sometimes the establishment of one's competence takes patience and diligence, as described by Charles Waldie, director of housing at Rutgers University: "When I first started as director of housing, the president, vice-presidents, and some deans were regularly making decisions that affected our operation, without consulting my office. They would react to complaints and issue directives to my office. To correct this, I requested from each violator the right to review any case before decisions were made. I was very careful to review these cases immediately and followed up immediately. Slowly I established competence and asserted the power of the division of housing. I had to be patient, but eventually I could regularly hear 'That's a housing problem; give it to the director' or 'What does the director of housing think about this?' "

This kind of competence requires being well prepared, according to Patrick Scheetz, assistant director of career development and placement services at Michigan State University: "So that I am included when top management is making decisions, it has been my habit to collect as much information . . . as possible on my subjects of career decision making, job-campaign planning, and job-market trends. Then, when university decisions are made, many of them affect my areas, and because I have these data, university administrators are likely to inquire about my perspective on these subjects."

In addition to establishing competence, effective leaders also project a "can do" attitude. As Charles Waldie of Rutgers notes, "I always try to say, 'Yes, we can do that' when the president or others in power make a request. In addition, I look for ways to solve any ongoing problems of the university, even if the problems are not totally related to housing." John Shingleton, director emeritus of placement services at Michigan State University, agrees: "When the university called upon me to handle any responsibility, I always gave an affirmative response. In carrying out these responsibilities, one earns a reputation, and if the reputation is positive, other responsibilities are offered." DePree (1989) notes that this type of management reflects a respect for the different gifts and potential of people. Waldie's and Shingleton's comments suggest their belief that organizations are well served by this attitude.

Jo Anne Trow, vice-president for student affairs at Oregon State University, provides an example of a "can do" attitude that resulted in a qualitative improvement. Her initial reaction to a proposal that her institution implement a total-quality management (TQM) project was "TQM? It will never work in student affairs! Why, it's just another way of looking at what we've been doing all along—another gimmick, with its own jargon that will take time to learn in an already crowded schedule. No, thank you. TQM is not for me." She goes on to say, "Those were the thoughts that ran through my mind when confronted with the mandate to learn more about and incorporate TQM into our operations. Skeptical as I was, however, I attended the workshops and read the materials. Before too long, I found myself less skeptical, willing to give it a try and implement it in the Division of Student Affairs at Oregon State University." The impact, she says, was great: "At Oregon State, it has positively influenced operations in admissions, financial aid, student housing and residence programs, college union programs and procedures, and career planning and placement. We are beginning applications in other areas and continuing [the] teams in the [aforementioned] units." Trow's experience illustrates how important it is to be open to new ideas and to have a "can do" attitude.

James Osteen, director of Stamp Student Union at the University of Maryland, College Park, agrees with this attitude and adds another dimension, related to broad-based thinking: "If I have been successful in being included in top-level management decisions, it is probably due in part to the following reasons. Whenever called upon to provide data, suggestions, solutions, or opinions for my supervisor or other top-level managers, I try to [ensure] that my parochial interests are represented yet stated in a manner that recognizes a broader perspective. I try to do my homework by discussing issues with persons who might understand the perspectives of my supervisor's colleagues, to whom he or she might have to justify a decision. I take assignments which give me the opportunity to work in a variety of settings on campus, to give me a broad view of issues. For example, I recently served on a search committee for two assistant bursars. Although the ultimate decisions had little to do with my department, my participation gave me the opportunity to work with a set of individuals from the administrative affairs area who represented a view of the campus much different from mine." This ability to think beyond one's own territory contributes to a leader's ability to have influence well beyond his or her functional unit.

Burns (1978) calls inclusion in this kind of institutional decision making "empowering." The leaders surveyed for this study continually affirm the importance of being involved in institutional issues beyond their own functional areas. As they relate, this kind of empowerment benefits them and their units. Anthony Adamo, dean of student life and development at Adelphi University, says, "If the chief student affairs officer expands his base of knowledge beyond student life issues and expresses, through words and actions, a willingness and commitment to assist in all facets of the university, there is a greater likelihood that he will be included in top-level management decisions. He must be strong and confident in supporting and challenging all areas of the university which significantly affect the student." Carmen Jordan-Cox, vice-president for student development at the University of San Francisco, concurs: "In order to be included in top management decisions, one has to do several things: have an implicit understanding of the informal as well as formal institutional network, know how to utilize both to get information and transmit it, and take the macrocosmic view of the university. One has to be able to understand how the parts make up the whole and what's best for the institution, not just one's own area of responsibility."

For Richard Stimpson of the University of Maryland, "being well informed, making myself available when needed, being willing to pick up responsibility for a share of the work necessary for implementation once a decision has been made—each helped facilitate my involvement in top-level decision making." He goes on to say, "Being informed—for example, knowing how the system works, being aware of key background developments, understanding the constraints associated with alternative courses of action, and so on—has helped ensure that I understand relevant issues, as well as previous developments, and will not ignorantly encourage an unwise course of action. I have found that it is best to be well informed before a decision-making session is initiated. When necessary, however, raising questions to gather needed information has been far wiser than being a silent or poorly informed participant."

Stimpson also comments on the importance of being available: "While we all have busy schedules and demanding work loads, being available—that is, taking steps to make myself available—has been an essential aspect of my recurring involvement in top-level decision making, particularly in times of crisis. While many decision-making sessions can be and are scheduled in advance, others are not. When a decision maker needs to pull folks together, he or she does not expect to have to personally deal with the problems that doing so may create. Availability can be facilitated by working out a plan for the rearrangement of calendars in advance. It is also wise to offer a follow-up explanation to those disrupted by last-minute changes in schedule. This helps ensure that the morale of others is not adversely affected by last-minute involvement in decision making." Stimpson emphasizes the importance of follow-up: "Many decisions result in the creation of extra work, and someone needs to do it. I have found that being willing to help focus how that work is going to be done and to share in getting it done has helped further my involvement in future decision-making sessions. Thinking out in advance how priorities can be rearranged and tasks can be delegated to others helps facilitate involvement in such implementation activities."

An additional ingredient of ensuring inclusion in institutional decision making is well articulated by Marsha Duncan, vice-president for student affairs at Lehigh University: "I believe that access to the inner circle, and therefore full participation in all major institutional decision making, is based on trust and loyalty. The president will engage those individuals whom he or she trusts and respects. Trust and respect are earned through hard work, clear thinking, effectiveness, and, most important, loyalty. There is no strategy on earth that will consistently ensure involvement in all major institutional decisions. I have the implicit and explicit trust of the president, and that alone is my ticket to the inner circle, where all major institutional decisions are made."

Effective leaders have a record of competence in their functional areas, and they extend their influence beyond their units. They see themselves as playing a role in institutional decision making. Establishing oneself in such a role takes patience, attention to detail, and preparation, as well as the willingness to handle additional responsibilities beyond the usual. Effective leaders also understand that the most important prerequisite for inclusion in institutional decision making is personal and institutional loyalty.

Involvement in the Budgeting Process

Institutional-level decisions increasingly involve budgetary dilemmas. Recent reports show fiscal conditions in state governments in 1991–1992 as being the "worst in a decade" (Blumenstyk and Crystal Cage, 1991), and projections are that the 1990s will bring further reductions in budgets for higher education (Hauptman, 1991). Leaders relish being involved in major institutional planning; they take advantage of the opportunity to be creative, and they involve their staff members in this important institutional process. This leads to what some experts on finance have heralded as an era of greater operational efficiency and an attitude of stronger reliance on innovation (Hauptman, 1991). Kuh and Nuss (1990) see this attitude as a mindset that views the continuously changing environment of higher education as challenging and inspiring, not threatening.

Maintaining perspective seems to be an important element of these leaders' involvement in budgeting. As the late Wayne Carlisle noted when he was at Wichita State University, "There are all kinds of budgeting years to experience during a career. The most useful approach to the bad year is to recognize the crunch is an experience shared by all parts of the university." In addition to recognizing the cyclical nature of budgeting, effective leaders also maintain an institutional, rather than a territorial, perspective. Margaret Barr of Texas Christian University recalls the wisdom of a colleague: "I think the basic approach that the provost at Lehigh used—saying that it does no good to say, 'The hole is not in my end of the canoe'—best describes my approach." Thomas Dutton of the University of California, Davis, agrees: "It is important to understand the needs of the rest of the campus. Student affairs cannot deal with budgetary problems in isolation."

Solid planning is very important in the budgeting process. Dutton advises, "The most important step is to have a sound strategic plan, with clearly stated goals and priorities. With such a plan, better budget decisions can be made in tight fiscal times." William Klepper of Trenton State College concurs, recommending "a planning process which assigns a value to each student affairs area, based on the institutional vision statement, and in turn measures the quality and demand of each program and service. These planning-process outcomes then allow resource allocation and any subsequent reorganization to be based on objective findings." Kuh and Nuss (1990) state that the student affairs organization that is successful in the budgeting process has a clear understanding of institutional mission and goals and is able to articulate efficiently how student affairs will contribute to the institution's educational processes. This type of planning ensures that resources will be allocated on the basis of educational purposes, and that there are sound and constructive debates on resource allocation (Barr, Upcraft, and Associates, 1990).

Discussing the concrete outcomes of this type of planning, Deborah Orr May, director of career planning and placement at the University of Michigan, maintains, "Planning should include mission reviews, environmental scans to determine opportunities, assessments of current strengths and weaknesses, and the willingness to add and delete services, based on assessments of quality, centrality, comparative advantage, and demand."

Leonard Goldberg, vice-president for student affairs at the University of Richmond, says that student affairs will need to be much more self-critical: "Many of us are facing situations where old assumptions regarding baseline operations and services need to be reexamined. Many overnight infirmaries, for example, have been shut down. Overnight care for the seriously ill is being delegated to hospitals, with the less ill being cared for in residence halls. Still other cases are sent home. For many campuses, [this] would have been unthinkable just a few years ago."

These leaders and others are saying that we cannot continue in an expansionist mode and that our decisions will need to be focused. Massey and Zemsky (1990) observe that higher education budgeting has built inflation into base budgets and has relied on inflationary increases to enable enhancements. They recommend "growth by substitution—a term that implies the need to achieve institutional excellence by developing more focused missions" (p. 1).

Where budgeting issues are concerned, leaders feel that one thing enabling their success is their ability to involve their staff members. Arthur Sandeen, vice-president for student affairs at the University of Florida, has found it useful "to involve staff members directly and share with them all information available." John Koldus, vice-president for student services at Texas A & M University, echoes this sentiment: "It's important to receive input from everyone and then base your priorities on sound, logical principles." Sandeen (1989) observes that it is quite natural for student affairs administrators to go to great lengths in order to be included in this type of decision making.

Such consultation and involvement are particularly important in times of budget reduction. Donald Adams, vice-president for enrollment management and student life at Drake University, says, "The total staff needs to have a part in the development of statements that will guide budget reductions and reorganization of services." Edward Webb, vice-president for student affairs at Humboldt State University, says, "Nothing succeeds better than consultation, involving those who will be affected by the cuts. If we hope to have our staffs buy into tough decisions, then they had better be part of the process." Margaret Barr of Texas Christian University acknowledges, "It is easier in the short run to do things uni- laterally, but in the long run it contributes to a sense of alien- ation from the process and reinforces the notion that 'they' are doing something to 'us' again." Kouzes and Posner (1987) advise leaders to involve those who must "live with the results" of decisions.

A national survey of chief student affairs officers ranked budgeting as second in importance among forty-four areas of expertise (Lunsford, 1984). Deegan (1981) states that budget- ing skills and the attendant political skills will become increas- ingly important as campuses work to retain campus authority in budgeting. Obviously, the leaders surveyed for this study agree. They demonstrate their effectiveness through the budgeting process. They maintain a solid institutional per- spective. They utilize a strategic planning process, which ensures that the student affairs agenda will be in harmony with institutional mission and goals. They use the budgeting process as a vehicle to involve their staff members in an impor- tant institutional function that can affect their morale and the outcomes of their work.

Reflections on Leaders' Thoughts

Effective leaders come from institutions that vary on every possible dimension—size, scope, student population, struc- ture, and locale. There seems to be no single type of institu- tion that best supports effective student services work. Leaders have identified some conditions, however, as important to their success. Leaders function best when the mission of the institution, whatever it is, is clear to all concerned. They find the environment supportive when there is congruence in the values expressed and exhibited by community members and when those values are congruent with their own. Leaders seek and enjoy inclusion in broad institutional decision making and take their roles in that process seriously, particularly their involvement in budgetary decisions. It is obvious that their influence extends beyond their own units. This influence is garnered because of their professional competence, their initiative and interest in larger campus issues, and their ready availability to campus colleagues when important issues are at hand.

This kind of leadership requires student affairs practitioners to act as "institutional officers." The positive outcomes are obvious: the voices and views of students are presented at the highest levels of decision making. This is a wonderful realization of student advocacy.

As the leaders surveyed for this study note, assuming this role requires time, effort, patience, and persistence. It also requires student affairs professionals—who generally relish working with students and running good units—to define their roles differently and spend more time with policy makers. While some practitioners may feel conflicted about this, as they progress in their careers they will need to adapt to a role that requires them to redefine what it means to serve students. This is not to say that spending time with students and running good units is not essential; it is not sufficient, however. Involvement in decision making is obviously a vital function that helps ensure that the development of students will remain the central mission of institutions of higher education. In fact, it may bring to our students' educational experience the congruence that Boyer (1987) identifies as so crucial.

PART TWO

Building
and
Maintaining
Relationships

CHAPTER FIVE

Interacting
with Students

Effective leaders in student services view interaction with students as a special privilege. They work diligently to establish and maintain relationships with students, and they note the breadth and the complexity of the roles involved.

Gary Althen, foreign student adviser at the University of Iowa, characterizes the wide-ranging roles he is called on to assume, noting that he functions "sometimes as a counselor, sometimes as an adviser, a writer, an editor, a trainer, teacher, supervisor, lawyer, administrator, and mentor. I probably would not want to do any one of these things all the time, but, in combination, they make for days that are unfailingly interesting." Effective leaders realize that they will vary their styles and roles as different situations and relationships with students develop, and they relish the opportunity to do so.

No matter what roles they assume, the leaders surveyed for this study list the following traits as essential to working with students: understanding and believing in students, communicating openly and challenging students appropriately, advocating for students, forming effective partnerships, and taking special care in relating to student leaders. All these traits and behaviors result in what is discussed in the literature as student affairs professionals' defining their priorities and goals in terms of both the student and the institution (Garland, 1985).

Understanding Students

Effective leaders understand the developmental processes so critical in students' lives and the importance of their role. Sara A. Boatman, former director of campus activities at the University of Nebraska, Lincoln, and currently chair of the department of communications and theater arts at Nebraska Wesleyan University, says, "Students are engaged in a continuous and cumulative process of development." She goes on to say that students' "age, gender, culture, and life experience affect their developmental processes, and the more I know about them, the better I can facilitate their growth."

Thomas Dutton, former vice-chancellor for student affairs at the University of California, Davis, affirms how important it is to understand students and the ways they are unique: "The most critical consideration has been to try to understand students' needs, motivations, goals, and priorities, and to keep in mind that they are unique individuals with different values, learning styles, and aspirations. It has been essential for me, in working with students over the years, to recognize these realities."

Rosalind Andreas, vice-president for student affairs, University of Vermont, also acknowledges how important it is to listen carefully if we are to honor the notion of diversity: "Somehow, we have to become far more proficient in listening to our many student bodies. As a profession, we state that each student is unique. The extent to which we can create enough comfort for students to begin to tell us in their own words how they experience our campuses from the perspective of their history, culture, identity—who they are—will probably determine how well we understand what our campuses do for and to students. Regrettably, I think we are still at a point where our campuses 'do things' to students rather than create environments which enhance belonging for students from differing cultural, ethnic, and religious backgrounds. We need to help our campuses change practices and programs, so that we find ways to create a sense of belonging for students with very different sets of experiences." Andreas recalls "a session with several Navajo students, when I asked them to help me understand how the campus made them feel. It created all kinds of conflict for them—with its competitive values, and its expectations of assertion and individualism. Navajo culture had taught them to look for harmony and balance through collaboration and cooperation. The campus rewarded competitiveness and assertion. They had been taught to avert their eyes from one in authority, out of respect. Professors expected successful students to disagree with them or question them—in direct conflict with tribal culture. I had to reevaluate my own reading of the nonverbal cue of eye contact. It suddenly took on new meaning for me." This example reinforces the point that personal and cultural diversity enriches our campuses if it is acknowledged and appreciated.

To understand students, leaders draw on their own experiences, as well as on the many theories available to educators today. Ronald Klepcyk, dean of student affairs at Elon College, believes that "student development theory can provide a basis for all that is done in a division of student affairs." Dennis Roberts, dean of students at Lynchburg College, supports the use of developmental theory: "We are truly eclectic, and, if we work at it, we can weave an integrated fabric of theories which complement one another and add tremendous power to our daily work."

Frank Ardaiolo, vice-president for student life at Winthrop College, talks about how theory permeates his practice: "Student development theory has always been important in my day-to-day roles. It helped me design programs when I was a primary service provider and has become more significant as my leadership role has broadened and as I have climbed up the career ladder. It is especially important in larger, complex organizations to maintain conceptual anchors to guide our managerial decisions as educators. Otherwise, we would be reduced to acting only out of expediency, or for what was cost-effective. The care for students and their development can be a remarkably strong anchor, even when the political storms around you—for they always occur, in any organization—are very threatening. As long as I have the ability to persist— and overcome some scarring in the process— my truly being able to articulate student development theory in everything I do will do the students, the institution, and me good."

Phyllis Mable, vice-president for student affairs at Longwood College, shares this appreciation of theory and draws heavily on it in interacting with students: "I believe that we teach students a certain kind of knowledge, skill, and attitude. Obviously, the knowledge, skill, and attitude come from theory. Our curriculum consists of concept and confidence development, community development (goals, responsibility, communication), care, and cooperation."

Richard Michael Paige, associate professor of international and intercultural education at the University of Minnesota, agrees: "I use theory constantly in my day-to-day role. For example, in planning an intercultural workshop, we review our expectations regarding learning outcomes in light of the literature, previous research findings, theoretical propositions, and past experience. We establish a conceptual foundation for everything we do. We draw attention to items in the literature for our staff to read. No single theory is all-embracing for our work; this field is inherently multi-disciplinary."

For the most part, when the leaders surveyed for this study talk about theories that they use in their work, they refer to student development theory, but is it important to note that other theories also have relevance to understanding students. Roger Campbell, dean of admissions, financial aid, and enrollment planning at the University of Denver, calls attention to that fact: "I have been intrigued by the way marketing theory can be adapted to admissions work and, indeed, to student personnel services as well. Marketing theory argues that you are engaged in the search for potential consumers who are a best match for your institution. Marketing theory requires the institution to assess itself. Therefore, the loop is completed. That is, by seeking students who have qualities that are well matched to the institution's set of dynamics, [we create] a considerable potential for growth . . . for both the student and the institution."

The leaders surveyed for this study have made a solid connection between theory and practice. They have found concrete ways to achieve the "developmental community" envisioned by Sanford (1966), a community that appropriately supports and challenges students and thereby enables development. Theory helps effective leaders understand students and organize their thinking about students, and it provides insights into approaches and courses of action (Knefelkamp, Parker, and Widick, 1989). For the leaders surveyed, developmental theories are a foundation of practice and a guide in shaping programs.

Besides using theory, effective leaders also acknowledge that their understanding of students is derived from their own personal involvement in the lives of students. C. Arthur Sandeen, vice-president for student affairs at the University of Florida, says, "I have never tried to rely on office contacts with students but to reach out to them, wherever they may be." The leaders surveyed for this study see opportunities to develop relationships with students as a special privilege. Alan Boyd, director of international student and faculty services at Ohio University, says, "Working with students and scholars, getting to know them, participating in what is for them a very significant experience, is very rewarding." He goes on to say that he is "constantly reminded of their personal diversity, and [I] feel honored to be able to be part of their lives, if even for a short time."

Leaders have a variety of approaches to establishing contact with students. As Boyd observes, "The most successful approach I have found is becoming involved in the lives of student leaders, showing appreciation for them as persons and as participants in activities. This process begins with orientation and continues throughout their careers on campus."

It is important to develop relationships over time, and many leaders spend time in places frequented by students. Donald Adams, vice-president for enrollment management and student life at Drake University, says, "The most successful approach in working with students is to meet often, and on their territory—their rooms, their offices, wherever they usually meet, rather than having them come to you." Tom Thielen, vice-president for student affairs at Iowa State University, notes the importance of "meeting them on their own turf by reaching out first or being accessible to them." Thomas Flynn, vice-president for student affairs at Monroe Community College, notes that informal contacts can be valuable: "I very much enjoy these free moments, when I can visit with students on matters of interest to them. It promotes a relationship that enhances better dialogue when [we have] to discuss issues of concern." The importance of these "walking around" contacts cannot be underestimated as a way of understanding students (Sandeen, 1991).

Other leaders surveyed for this study develop relationships with students through more structured approaches. Dorothy Anderson, dean of students at Susquehanna University, stresses finding ways to stay in direct touch with students and student groups: "For me, that translates into being the adviser to the Student Government Association; advising Alpha Lambda Delta [the freshman honor society]; meeting on a weekly basis with the campus newspaper's news editor; eating some meals in the cafeteria; attending sports events, plays, and recitals; and talking with and listening to students. Life can get so busy, with administrative tasks, committee assignments, meetings, and so on, that it can be all too easy to lose touch with students, the very reason for being in this profession."

John Koldus, vice-president for student services at Texas A & M University, lends a relaxed tone to formal meetings. He says, "The Europeans—I'm of Hungarian heritage—have a tendency to do things in association with food. People tend to relax, to be more sociable than confrontational, and so I use this technique a great deal. My student leaders have dinner with me each Thursday. The president and I meet with student leaders twice a semester for lunch. I host a lunch series each week, involving about twenty-two people—freshmen alone, upperclassmen alone, and one with students, faculty, and staff. I also have food functions at my home on campus and take students to lunch at the Faculty Club."

Some leaders stress both formal as well as informal approaches to meetings with students. John McCray, Jr., vice-president for student development at the University of Rhode Island, says, "My interactions with students and student groups are both formal and informal. A formal meeting, usually scheduled at the beginning of the academic year, allows for due process in handling complaints and concerns from students. It is visible and effective in providing students and their groups access to university leadership. Informal meetings include those that are planned in conjunction with my schedule and the students' schedules and those that occur as I wander around campus. There is a place for both types of communication, and so one should not be deemed more important than the other."

Effective practitioners need to maintain relationships with students through formal and informal methods. It is essential for all student affairs administrators to stay in touch with students on an individual basis (Upcraft and Barr, 1988).

Developing Open and Honest Relationships

Effective leaders develop open and honest relationships with students that are characterized by mutual trust and respect and by the acknowledgment that, in the educational process, they have a unique partnership with students. The leaders surveyed for this study note that believing in, valuing, and caring for students are at the core of their relationships with students. Donald Perigo, ombudsman at the University of Michigan, discusses how important attentiveness is to his work: "The approach that has worked best for me is believing that each group has value, and its members are the people most important to me at that time. I try very hard to be an active listener and, if offering assistance, promise my best but not necessarily success." Leonard Goldberg, vice-president for student affairs at the University of Richmond, characterizes staff members who are effective in their relationships with students as "able to communicate, in tangible and intangible ways, that they appreciate and like students and respect their abilities and intellect." David Ostroth, director of student activities at Virginia Polytechnic Institute and State University, shares this perspective and believes that "to be really successful in this field, you have to really like students. I think it's extremely important that we have empathy for students, their concerns, and the stresses they are feeling in the college environment." Others, writing on this topic, have stressed the importance of caring in winning the confidence and support of students (see Sandeen, 1991). A caring relationship involves listening to and legitimizing the student's voice with basic trust, believing that the student's voice must be heard and empowered, and understanding how students' values and needs fit in with institutional issues (Knefelkamp, 1981).

When leaders believe in students and identify with their concerns, they are able to be direct and honest—two characteristics that are highly valued by all concerned. James Grimm, director of housing at the University of Florida, endorses this point of view: "I believe that it is imperative that we deal honestly and openly with students and/or student groups. My approach has always been to consider students as reasonable and intelligent individuals. Therefore, dealing with them honestly and openly usually has rational, reasonable, and mutually acceptable results." George Preisinger, director of the university center and campus activities at the University of Maryland, Baltimore County, concurs: "I strive for honesty in my relations with students. There is no advantage to making students guess at my position or viewpoint; it does little but foster ambiguity, engender mistrust, and waste time." Thomas Dutton of the University of California, Davis, says, "We need to be candid and truthful in explaining both personal and institutional positions and priorities."

Many of the leaders surveyed for this study caution against any kind of deceit or manipulation. Margaret Bridwell, director of the student health center at the University of Maryland, College Park, believes that it is important "to be up front with students. I try very hard to tell them the truth, not manipulate them, and say that I can't tell them something, rather than make up a story. I try to treat them as adults, with respect, and explain whatever they want in terms they can understand. If I am in error, I say so and try not to be defensive." Robert Minetti, vice-president for student affairs at Bentley College, puts this admonition succinctly: "Students will forgive incompetence and ignorance, but never lie to them!" Larry Moneta, associate vice-provost for university life at the University of Pennsylvania, shares this perspective: "Students have a remarkable ability to see right through deceit and manipulation by administrators. They recognize a patronizing attitude and will quickly reject any collaborative relationships with administrators who engage in deceit."

Open, honest relationships sometimes require administrators to deliver bad news. Donald Gwinn, registrar at Northwestern University, acknowledges that relationships between people with different levels of power, although complex, can be made less so when the people relate to each other with candor: "I suppose an inherent suspicion of authority builds up in every young person during adolescence. Any impression that an administrator is less than honest or trying to put one over is not received at all well. Even in situations where the news is not good for the student, if an attitude of helpfulness is apparent, the relationship can remain good." Thomas Carver, vice-president for student affairs and dean of students at Berry College, echoes the sentiment that "helpfulness is important." He says, "One's approach should be characterized by an attitude of 'How can I be of help?'" When effective leaders deliver bad news, they extend themselves and offer to help in appropriate ways.

Other leaders surveyed for this study also acknowledge that students can hear bad news, and they accept responsibility for their own roles in situations that are not completely positive. Leonard Goldberg of the University of Richmond says, "Open relationships are not always smooth." He adds, "Open relationships should not be confused with always agreeing." Margaret Barr, vice-president for student affairs at Texas Christian University, says it is best "to approach students with honesty, and to try not to fool them in any way. If they are in trouble, for example, they need to know the consequences of their actions, but they also need to know that we are judging their behavior, not them as human beings."

Leaders acknowledge the importance of explaining fully to students their reasons for disagreeing or denying requests. Stuart Sharkey, vice-president for student affairs at the University of Delaware, says, "Students do not tolerate administrators' runaround and jargon. If you have the time to explain your position, there is a better chance of its being accepted, even if you have to deny a student's request or disagree with a student's idea. Too often, administrators simply say no because it's policy. Students are quick to determine genuineness."

To summarize, effective leaders develop candid relationships with students, never attempting to deceive or manipulate them. Candid relationships do not entail protecting students from critical feedback, but they do mean delivering it with full information and in a way that respects human dignity.

Advocating for Students

Effective leaders see themselves as advocates for students. Jacoby (1991) notes that advocacy has a broad definition: it may involve tasks as complex as forming and managing advisory boards and as simple as placing a telephone call on behalf of a student with a problem. Edward Webb, vice-president for student affairs at Humboldt State University, shares this perspective: "Individual students have a need to know someone in the administration who listens, who cares, who advocates and is fair." Dorothy Anderson of Susquehanna University agrees: "In order to be effective, it is important to continually represent the best interests of students in the context of the whole university."

A study of effective deans of students (Appleton, Briggs, and Rhatigan, 1978) emphasizes how important it is for students to advocate for themselves and have input into the policies and procedures that affect them. Through their understanding and the strength of their relationships, leaders expand on their roles as advocates by empowering students. Rob Rouzer, director of Wilson Commons/Student Activities at the University of Rochester, says, "Students generally approach administrators with the expectation of 'the administration' taking some action to meet their perceived problem. I've found that students are most successful, and ultimately most satisfied, when I can show them the way to solve problems themselves." Phyllis Mable of Longwood College says, "I always want students to know that I expect them to be responsible—to take responsibility, and to accomplish tasks in responsible ways. Expecting responsibility—choice, involvement, performance—is important as students learn how to be leaders."

Finding balance in these relationships is important in helping students take responsibility. Neal Gamsky, vice-president and dean of student affairs at Illinois State University, says, "With student leaders, my role has been that of consultant or adviser, and not that of a surrogate parent or an involved, uncaring bureaucrat." Ernest L. Bebb, director of the student union at the University of Utah, talks about an essential element of such balanced relationships: "commitment to assisting students to be their own strong and effective advocates, instead of trying to be direct advocates for them." He also mentions "feeling comfortable letting them know where we differ, when necessary, while assuring them that I will help them seek their goals in whatever way I believe I can, without compromising myself or my responsibility to represent the best interests of the institution." Gamsky agrees:

"We do them a disservice educationally by trying to do too much *for* them. On most campuses, they have the skills, resources, and power necessary to be their own advocates on most issues. They do, however, need to be assisted to take the initiative and to assume responsibility for their behavior."

The leaders surveyed for this study are certainly advocates for students, but they see an even more important role for themselves: teaching students how to be advocates for themselves. Some caution that if institutions do not allow students to become their own advocates, the students will not develop leadership skills and will not feel a sense of ownership (Sandeen, 1991).

Relating to Student Leaders

As is evident, effective leaders emphasize the importance of understanding students and developing relationships with students throughout their institutions. While leaders value these wide-ranging relationships, they also note that developing strong relationships with particular student leaders and groups is key to their success. Two key student leaders on any campus are the student government president and the editor of the student newspaper.

The leaders surveyed for this study begin their relationships with these student leaders with the belief that student leaders are an important part of the institutional power structure. William Brattain, assistant vice-president for student services at Western Illinois University, says, "We need to continue to serve as advocates for student participation in the university governance process." Tim Gallineau, vice-president for student development at Saint Bonaventure University, calls on us to "be assertive in making sure students are actively participating in all aspects of university governance." David Horner, director of the Office for International Students and Scholars at Michigan State University, says that we ensure this outcome by "facilitating meetings in ways that encourage group participation, involvement, and eventually ownership of the issues." Walter Gilliard, associate dean of students at the University of Dayton, offers the example of "sharing with individual student leaders limited administrative functions indigenous to their organizational budgets and their responsibility as leaders." These suggestions entail being willing to share control of the institution with students and realizing that there are many ways to achieve institutional purposes, some of which institutional administrators may not have considered (Kuh, Schuh, Whitt, and Associates, 1991).

Student Government Leaders

Student governments manage large sums of money, represent students on a wide array of committees, and sometimes play a role in lobbying external bodies (Lawson, 1981). These organizations and their leaders obviously have the ability to influence the nature and quality of student life and student affairs programs. Donald Adams of Drake University notes that "a familiarity of common goals, shared perceptions, working together on common tasks, but, most important, mutual respect for a partner in the student government president's position" all enhance the ability to work with these student leaders. An important step in facilitating mutuality is to gain an understanding of what student government leaders need. Carmen Jordan-Cox, vice-president for student development at the University of San Francisco, says, "Take some time to get to know the needs of your student government president, and structure opportunities for him or her to meet these needs. He or she will appreciate this and respect you as a person and as a professional."

Sharing a sense of collegiality with student leaders is identified as important. Thomas Carver of Berry College notes, "I find it essential to be in touch with that person, and sometimes all officers of the student government association, in a personal meeting at least once a week. I also attend all student government association meetings, which does much to enhance credibility. Having also been a student government president, and sharing some of those experiences from time to time with students, also help in that misery loves company."

Roger Morris, associate director of student development at the University of Oregon, expands on the notion of collegiality: "In our office, we invite the student body president to our staff meetings. We are also the only office in the student affairs division that shares weekly staff minutes." Carmen Jordan-Cox says, "The key here is treating the student government president as a quasi-member of your staff. This involves laying out clear expectations and principles (including integrity, openness, confidentiality, and trust) for your working relationship. He or she needs opportunities to show that he or she can deliver and have an impact on the governance structure and management decisions." Dennis Golden, vice-president for student affairs at the University of Louisville, agrees: "Bring the SGA [student government association] into a full partnership regarding meetings and governance. SGA presidents should be *voting* members of the board of trustees. They should also be present at and partners in major and regular meetings of student life and student development professionals."

Establishing a collegial relationship should not diminish the educational role that leaders play with student government leaders. Effective practitioners must be concerned about working with these students to identify strategies that will lead to a strong, responsible student association and a wide array of intentional, developmental experiences (Lawson, 1981). The leaders surveyed for this study agree. As Dennis Golden says, "Remember that SGA presidents are students first, last, and always." He adds, "Assist them and guide them through the bureaucratic red tape, and don't let them harm their academic careers or personal health and well-being."

In their role as educators, effective leaders note that this is made more difficult by the transience of student government leaders. As William Brattain of Western Illinois University says, "Keep in mind that each year brings a new individual, and what worked with the previous administration may have to be changed with the new one." He also emphasizes how important this experience may be for the individual student government leader: "It is important to keep in perspective that this one year is very important in the life of this elected student official, and although we have read some of the proposals before, it is the first time it has come from this individual."

Relationships with student government leaders take many forms. Formal relationships are enhanced by informal interaction. "Approachable, accessible, and interested" are terms that Edward Webb of Humboldt State uses to characterize his style with student government leaders: "It helps to drop by their offices occasionally and chat, if only to ask about how they are doing in school, what projects they are working on, or how their vacations were." Frank Julian, former vice-president for student development at Murray State University, has an innovative approach to facilitating informal interactions: "I provided apartments for the SGA leadership in my building (a renovated residence hall). They were ecstatic, and I get to use their proximity to stay in constant touch with them."

At the heart of these relationships is the motivation to truly hear from student government leaders. James Quann, registrar at the University of California, Santa Cruz, says that he likes "to have their input" on serious issues facing his institution and likes "to discuss pending policy changes or new innovations under consideration. I also ask for their endorsement of important projects or initiatives." As a result, Quann says, "we will more likely than not discover we have allies in whatever it is we are trying to accomplish." Making allies should not be confused with co-opting student government leaders. Dennis Golden of the University of Louisville cautions us to "never use the SGA as a power or a means to an end, to get what you want or need." He adds the thought that student government leaders need the freedom to risk: "Each SGA has the right and needs the opportunity to do its own thing its way. Always remember and believe that student governments have the right to succeed *and* the right to fail. If they can't do this *with safety* in college, they may never be able to do it." Thus, effective leaders seek the input and endorsement of student government leaders and are careful not to manipulate or distort their involvements and relationships.

All the perspectives offered by the leaders surveyed for this study reflect a belief in the importance of the role of student government in the institutional governance process. These leaders emphasize the idea that we need to work with students to overcome inertia and disorganization. Some writers note that students lack decision-making authority, cohesiveness, continuity, and formalized training (Downey, 1981); the leaders surveyed for this study believe that this does not have to be the case if student government leaders can be supported, legitimized, and drawn into the institutional governance process.

Student Newspaper Editors

A second student leader identified as critical is the editor of the student newspaper. Phyllis Mable of Longwood College says, "Taking a real interest in the student newspaper editor is essential." The student newspaper represents values that academic communities hold dear: freedom of speech, inquiry, and expression; the search for truth; concern for the community and the common good (Schuh, 1986). Therefore, effective leaders in student services give attention and support to student newspaper editors. The leaders surveyed for this study use some of the same techniques and approaches that they use with student government leaders, but they stress the importance of establishing clear guidelines about roles and having direct lines of communication.

Participants in this study and researchers in the field alike note that our responsibilities as educators also extend to those special student leaders. Schuh (1986), writing about enhancing relationships with the student press, presents these relationships as opportunities to teach reporters and the larger campus about student affairs work. The leaders surveyed for this study also note the importance of seeing these students as learners. James Lyons, dean emeritus of student affairs at Stanford University, says, "Newspaper editors [have] rarely edited newspapers before. If they knew how to do that, they would (or should) be moving on to other things. So they are learning, and I do what all educators do: I try to support their learning and be helpful whenever possible." This is not always easy. As Raymond Heath, vice-president for student affairs at La Salle University, says, "Years ago, it was easier to forget that these students were learning, and that a teaching role should be emphasized to a greater degree than an ownership role with respect to the publication they had responsibility for." Heath is alluding, of course, to the difficulty of playing the educator's role when a student editor is assuming an aggressive or hostile position toward the administrator. Administrators can feel the conflict of being educators and simultaneously being accountable for the institution's image (DeCoster and Krager, 1986).

A number of solid ideas have emerged for getting this relationship off to a positive start. James Lyons says, "Once or twice annually, I entertain the editorial staff in my home, along with other university folks who are often called by the press: the president, the provost, the police chief, another dean or two, the registrar, several members of my staff, the athletic director, and one or two members of the university news and publications staff." He says that this "helps the students connect names and faces—to humanize the process, and vice versa."

Meeting and facilitating relationships with others in authority is widely hailed as good practice. Herman Kissiah, dean of students at Lafayette College, says, "With respect to establishing effective working relationships with student leaders, such as the newspaper editor or student government leaders, I have followed the practice of having lunch every Friday of the academic year with two individuals and the president of our fraternity and sorority organization. This meeting gives the four of us an opportunity to get to know each other as individuals and as persons representing different organizations and offices. The meetings are often as useful for the student leaders in getting to know one another as for me in getting to know them, or for them in getting to know me. On some Fridays, the discussions are directly related to current college issues. On other Fridays, the focus may be on issues which are less taxing or less controversial. On weekends when the board of trustees is meeting, I invite several trustees to join me for my Friday luncheon groups." Both Lyons and Kissiah stress how student affairs leaders can facilitate relationships of newspaper editors and other leaders with the institution's administrative leaders.

Meeting regularly involves some educational goals but also some pragmatic ones. As Kissiah notes about his regular Friday luncheons with the newspaper editor, "The college newspaper appears on Friday morning, and one of the responsibilities of the editor is to bring a copy of the paper to the meeting. While waiting for lunch to be served, we usually take a quick look at the paper, in order to see what the editor might think are the important issues, and to see if we have been quoted correctly or [if] our names [are] misspelled. Perhaps it is an unfair advantage, but the editors with whom I have worked have often found it difficult to castigate me in an editorial and then expect me to pay for lunch immediately after reading about myself." Although certainly offered with a sense of humor, this kernel of wisdom concerns the importance of establishing a personal connection to ensure fair treatment by newspaper editors.

Personally extending oneself and institutional resources is an important theme. As Stuart Sharkey of the University of Delaware says, "I arrange to have lunch with the [student newspaper editor]. I offer to participate in the training program of his or her staff, and I invite the editor to be on my undergraduate cabinet, composed of student leaders and class representatives." Effective practitioners, through extensions of themselves, involve student editors in forums for student and institutional leadership.

This extension of self may cross personal boundaries. Sharkey says, "I am always available to reporters and to the editor. Reporters should feel free to call me in the evening and on weekends." Samuel Sadler, vice-president for student affairs at the College of William and Mary, says, "The newspaper staff has access to me whenever they need it. I give key editors my home phone number and urge them to use it at any time." James Lyons of Stanford says succinctly, "I am always available to be called—any hour." This willingness to be contacted at home shows how important student newspaper editors are to effective practitioners.

All those who have commented note the importance of honesty but have different feelings about speaking off the record. Stuart Sharkey relates, "I promise the editor that I will never mislead anyone, and if I cannot discuss an issue, I will tell the reporter up front that it is not possible." James Lyons says one of his ground rules is that he will "never talk off the record. If I can't talk, I'll say so. I'll always be forthright; no half-truths." By contrast, Sadler comments, "If I have a concern about how the information might be used, I ask to speak off the record and explain my concerns. That candor has never been violated." Whether statements are on or off the record, leaders emphasize being clear about one's style and expectations. Whatever the style, says James Grimm of the University of Florida, "always be honest, even if it hurts." He adds, "I have found that I have gotten myself or my department in trouble when I tried to hedge on this or that item. Therefore, I have tried to be responsive, honest, and factual, even saying, 'I don't know' or 'That is not within my jurisdiction.' This seems to be the most practical approach to at least keeping your foot out of your mouth." DeCoster and Krager (1986) share the perspectives of the leaders surveyed for this study, cautioning that, regardless of motivation, the distortion or submersion of information almost always engenders distrust and controversy.

William Johnston, assistant vice-president for student affairs at Southern Methodist University, also emphasizes candor and the importance of understanding the role of the student press. He says that good relationships with the student press can be enhanced "by candor, openness, and a proven concern for First Amendment rights; by [the] understanding that the student paper is not a publicity organ for the university and has editorial and operational needs which transcend the [public relations] needs of the institution; and, finally, by [the] understanding that these folks are developing and learning and will make mistakes, even when it is my ox that is being gored."

The techniques that work with other people work with student editors, too. David Ross, associate dean of student affairs at Central Connecticut University, says, "Communication is important." Dorothy Pijan, director of the Thwing Center at Case Western Reserve University, agrees: "As in . . . most [other] human relationships, nothing can beat daily communication and an understanding and interested attitude."

Leaders identified the editor of the student newspaper as an important campus leader. They noted the importance of seeing these leaders as learners, but recognized that this can be difficult when controversial concerns arise on campus.

Forming Partnerships

From these efforts to teach students, assist them, and facilitate their taking responsibility, leaders come to view these relationships as partnerships. David Butler, director of housing and residence life at the University of Delaware, says, "Student affairs must form partnerships with students, teach them skills, and trust them to lead appropriately." Donald Adams of Drake University says, "Accepting students as full partners and colleagues in the university setting is crucial." Laurence Smith, vice-president for university marketing and student affairs at Eastern Michigan University, subscribes to the partnership idea but adds, "I see students as legitimate partners, but I also feel it is a legitimate and necessary part of my role to help bridge the gap between their inexperience and my professional knowledge and expertise." The effective leaders surveyed for this study go beyond the educator's role and acknowledge students as colleagues, partners, and major actors in shaping their own education and the educational milieu.

Reflections on Leaders' Thoughts

The leaders surveyed for this study value their relationships with students. They believe that it is important to work hard to understand students and develop open and honest communication. They see student advocacy as an important responsibility, but they also see themselves as partners with students, and they take special care to establish strong relationships with key student leaders.

As the leaders talk about their relationships with students, the complexity of these relationships is apparent. For many students, the college years are tumultuous ones developmentally. The umbrella term *students* seems wholly inadequate as a label for a group of people with so many subgroups and individual differences. The task of listening carefully and analyzing how these differences are supported or obscured in the campus environment is daunting. Nevertheless, it is one of the essential tasks of an effective student affairs practitioner.

In addition to the complexity of the students themselves, student affairs professionals must also contend with the challenge of role definition. Not only do they assume multiple and sometimes conflicting roles, they also have the responsibility of advocacy for people with whom they simultaneously want to form partnerships, which assumes a level of equality.

It is easy to see why the relationships of student affairs practitioners with students are challenging, demanding, perplexing, and energizing. When the right fit is established, these relationships flourish, with partnerships that energize students, student affairs practitioners, and institutions.

CHAPTER SIX

Enlisting Faculty Support

The leaders surveyed in this study uniformly believe that there are some essential elements of good relationships with faculty members, especially understanding and valuing the centrality of the role of the faculty. Effective leaders realize the potential of faculty-staff relationships, realistically acknowledge the obstacles, and use a variety of approaches to forging meaningful partnerships.

Relationships with Faculty Members

Writing about the historical foundations of student services, Fenske (1989) notes how important it is for student services practitioners to recognize that teaching, learning, and research are the primary missions of higher education. The leaders surveyed for this study concur. Thomas Carver, vice-president for student affairs at Berry College, says that good relationships with faculty members begin with the recognition "that the academic area is the central mission of the college." Donald Adams, vice-president for enrollment management and student life at Drake University, agrees: "The instructional program of the university is why the students come to a college or university." Thomas Dutton, former vice-chancellor for student affairs at the University of California, Davis, says, "Student affairs staff must begin with an understanding of the institution's academic mission and the critical role of the faculty in implementing that mission. In my judgment, the faculty must be seen as the core of the academic enterprise, with student affairs playing a vital complementary role. With this perspective, I feel that it is possible to establish effective working relationships with the faculty." As partners in the educational enterprise, student affairs professionals can enhance the academic mission (Fenske, 1989; Brown, 1989).

Others share Dutton's perspective that student affairs has a complementary role to play, and they relish that role. Adams says, "What I love to do is be supportive of the chief academic affairs officer and help build an environment where learning can take place." This does not mean that student affairs practitioners are subservient. Leonard Goldberg, vice-president for student affairs at the University of Richmond, says, "We need to believe in our mission and to be realistic about it. . . . The academic mission of the institution is preeminent. If we keep that assumption in perspective, it will help guide us in the way we relate to the faculty and the students."

Betty Suddarth, registrar of Purdue University, describes this support of the academic mission in very concrete terms: "Student affairs staff must recognize that they have a responsibility to support the academic mission of the university and participate as team players. The role of the registrar is closely related to [that of] the faculty in that most services provide the necessary out-of-class administrative functions required to allow the in-class functions to operate smoothly. Determining who is registered for a given class, recording that registration, collecting grades, maintaining and providing information on academic history, and providing student summary information are all necessary functions that the faculty needs to have accomplished. Assisting the faculty in establishing academic policies and regulations for the benefit of the institution and its students is another way to develop meaningful relationships with faculty." Suddarth clearly sees the supportive role that student services can play for the faculty. Appleton, Briggs, and Rhatigan (1978) note that "competency" in providing services is a key to making contacts with the faculty positive. The importance of this supportive role is also affirmed by the National Association of Student Personnel Administrators (1987). With a firm commitment to the centrality of the academic mission, student services staff respect the critical role of the faculty and strive to provide the administrative support that will enable the faculty and the academic enterprise to flourish.

The leaders surveyed for this study agree that the foundation for relationships with the faculty must be an understanding of the faculty's important role in accomplishing the primary aims of the institution. Beyond this affirmation, there are divergent viewpoints among these leaders on the potential of relationships between student affairs practitioners and the faculty. Some describe the obstacles to forming relationships. Some stress the opportunities for student affairs practitioners to develop partnerships with the faculty. Some feel that there are gains to be made in blurring the lines between the groups. Comments from leaders who hold these three basic views follow.

Obstacles

Gary Althen, foreign student adviser at the University of Iowa, says, with wry humor, "I do not believe it is always possible for student affairs staff to develop meaningful relationships with the faculty. It seems to me that some faculty are so imbued with the notion that they represent a superior form of life that staff members cannot develop meaningful relationships with them. A possible exception is the case of the staff member who has a Ph.D. in the faculty member's discipline, graduated from the faculty member's alma mater (or a more highly regarded school), and subscribes to the same methodological faiths that the faculty member does."

It can be difficult to establish credibility when one's credentialing process is different. In some measure, the credibility issue for student affairs professionals may stem from what Kerr and Gade (1986) call an "antiadministration" attitude on the part of some faculty members. Another obstacle may be practitioners' own feelings about working with the faculty. Creeden (1989) feels that student affairs staff do have prejudices, which they must abandon if they wish to increase collaboration between academic and student affairs. David Butler, director of housing and residence life at the University of Delaware, acknowledges that practitioners may have to overcome their timidity and take steps to ensure their own involvement: "If we really want to expand interactions, we are first, as a profession, going to have to stop being afraid of the faculty and, second, we are going to have to realize that the faculty is valuable and budget for faculty involvement with students."

Peter Rea, assistant academic dean, formerly director of career services, at Baldwin-Wallace College, says that faculty members have a different perspective, and he offers a cultural characterization of the differences: "In some ways, we are talking about two different cultures. The temperament, values, training, responsibilities, and roles of the faculty and student service administrators are quite different. The faculty and student services professionals tend to operate in different worlds. Faculty members spend time in their classrooms, offices, and committee meetings, primarily involved in teaching, research, and service. Student affairs professionals spend time in their offices, residence halls, and committee meetings, counseling and programming for students and administering a range of student services. One world attracts introverts, who are devoted to specialized scholarship and student learning. The other world attracts extroverts, who are devoted to student development." Paul Moore, vice-president for student affairs at California State University, Chico, concurs: "In the main, faculty members will be concerned with other things, their own things, and not ours, and we shouldn't try to force an unreasonable agenda on the faculty and expect the faculty to be particularly concerned with our issues." Green (1988) also states that most faculty members prefer to be left alone by administrators.

Peter Rea adds that, although his comparisons "oversimplify the differences between faculty and administrators, the point is to underscore that for administrators to develop meaningful relationships with the faculty will take significant effort and expertise. Unfortunately, there is too little overlap between the two camps. Too few faculty members administer, and too few administrators teach and conduct research. Academic issues are frequently misunderstood by nonteaching administrators. Student affairs issues are frequently misunderstood by the faculty."

It does not suffice to acknowledge the differences; student affairs professionals must understand the faculty's values and culture. William Klepper, dean of student life at Trenton State College, explains, "The formula for success in developing meaningful relationships with the faculty is a fuller understanding of the academic life-style." Charles Schroeder, vice-president for student services at Georgia Institute of Technology, reflects, "Student affairs staff members need to understand faculty culture—its values, priorities, language, and biases. Student affairs staff members should focus their efforts on helping the faculty be more effective and successful." Understanding faculty culture is particularly complex because the American professoriate has evolved into a profession with multiple cultures (Boyer, 1987).

The cultures of the faculty and student affairs are significantly different. As Creeden (1989) indicates, it is important to note that faculty and staff members have different roles to play, but both roles demonstrate commitment to students. Time, effort, and expertise are necessary for the development of faculty-staff relationships.

A Partnership

Some leaders stress the importance of finding common ground in building relationships. According to Laurence

N. Smith, vice-president for university marketing and student affairs at Eastern Michigan University, "We must be able to clearly articulate our vision and values and invite faculty members and others to work with us to achieve them. We must also participate in helping them achieve their vision. There must be many bridges built, professionally and programmatically, socially and politically. While there are key differences in the work we do, we ultimately have the same goals of producing a quality work, living, and learning environment. I truly believe that, regardless of how many differences separate us, there are more things that unite us in a university community." Frank Julian, former vice-president for student development at Murray State University, identifies the elements that unite: "I find that most faculty members care very much about the academic and personal success of their students. Therefore, I've always felt as though we're 'playing from the same page of the playbook,' as a friend of mine used to say. I always emphasize the mutuality of our goals for students when working with the faculty. . . . I think we too often perpetuate the idea of a gap between faculty and staff members, which may not exist on all campuses."

Roger Wehrle, director of the student center and auxiliary enterprises at Georgia Institute of Technology, shares this perspective on common goals: "To develop a meaningful relationship, I think the teaching faculty must view not only student affairs staff but all administrative staff personnel as peers in a common goal. We can achieve this by getting to know them on a personal basis and at the same time constantly communicating to them the value of our services to the students and to them as individual faculty members."

The outcome can be solid partnerships, which will require faculty and staff members to interact in significant ways (Miller, Winston, and Associates, 1991). Margaret Barr, vice-chancellor for student affairs at Texas Christian University, says, "I have always assumed that we are partners in the higher education enterprise and also assume that faculty members are as interested as I am in developing relationships that challenge and support them." Barr's assumption emphasizes commonality rather than differences.

Patricia Kearney, assistant vice-chancellor for student affairs at the University of California, Davis, brings up some ideas about how staff members can begin to establish partnerships: "If we keep waiting to be asked to dance, we will never be able to develop meaningful relationships with the faculty. Are we willing to share our turf with the faculty? If we are willing to ask the faculty to participate meaningfully in planning and developing the student services agenda, meaningful relationships will follow." Kearney asks the difficult question of how open student affairs practitioners are to involvements that go well beyond the "guest appearances" we often request of faculty members.

William Klepper of Trenton State College uses a practical example to illustrate what it takes to form such partnerships: "I am firm in my belief that the future of student affairs is in the linkage of the academic and student affairs enterprises. My first thought, as I venture into new programs, is 'How can this effort be brokered to the faculty and academic leaders of the campus?' There is success in giving up in order to get. Let me be specific. For years, our division ran an orientation event for entering students. The program was successful, but the involvement of the faculty and academic leaders was minimal. The recommendation was to redefine orientation, from an *event* to a *process* made up of seven elements. It would begin with a spring reception for prospective students and conclude with the existing College Seminar course at the end of the first semester. In between, there would be a basic-skills and mathematics-placement testing program, an advisement week to replace the traditional summer orientation, a summer reading program, a welcome week prior to the beginning of the academic year, and a formal convocation, with full academic regalia. In each element, there is direct faculty involvement with students—we gave up one event, and in return we got a comprehensive academic–student affairs program for supporting the students' transition into our community of learners." Klepper reaffirms Patricia Kearney's point: that we must be willing to share our turf with faculty members if we hope to enlist their true involvement.

Klepper is at peace with assuming more than his fair share of work in eliciting collaborative relationships with the faculty, and so are others. Deborah Orr May, director of career planning and placement at the University of Michigan, says, "To develop meaningful relationships with the faculty, we have to be willing to initiate the relationships and probably do the majority of the legwork, at least initially. This would allow us, just like the Little Prince and the fox, to sit a little bit closer to each other every day, until we begin to establish genuine relationships. One good way to do this is to work collaboratively on a project over time. Once a relationship has been established—once mutual respect has been developed—we are able to hear each other and can be open to learn from each other." May's perspective is also found in Reger and Hyman (1989), which notes many examples of collaborative relationships between faculty and staff members, generally initiated by student affairs practitioners. Kearney, Klepper, and May stress that developing relationships with the faculty requires patience, time, and energy. The payoff is practitioners' own enhanced ability to meet students' educational needs (Fenske, 1989).

Effective leaders use a variety of approaches to establishing good working relationships with faculty members. First and foremost, it is essential to spend time with them. John Schuh, associate vice-president for student affairs at Wichita State University, says, "One of the best things I do each year is try to meet with each new faculty member in her or his office, just to get acquainted and say a little bit about student affairs. The response I get from this effort is phenomenal. By the way, this idea is not original with me; Bob Shaffer used to do this when he was dean at Indiana." Margaret Barr of Texas Christian University also takes this activist approach: "Get out and about with the faculty," she advises. "Staying in your office, or only associating with students, does not help build bridges. Eat lunch where faculty members do. Attend all faculty meetings, when it is appropriate. Go to departmental and collegiate functions when you are asked. Be accessible and available to the faculty."

Donald Adams of Drake University agrees with Schuh: "It is very important to take time to meet faculty members where they gather, such as at seminars, faculty dining rooms, or faculty meetings." Samuel Sadler, vice-president for student affairs at the College of William and Mary, recalls, "Over the years, my most effective relationships with faculty members have come about in two ways. First, I serve on as many faculty committees as I can, and, second, I attend and participate in faculty meetings. This gives me an opportunity to show my interest in and support for academic issues, and it gives the faculty a chance to learn about me and the quality of my judgment and about the ways in which my staff and I can support the academic enterprise." These leaders have obviously become a resource to faculty members, a role whose importance has been stressed by the National Association of Student Personnel Administrators (1987).

Jean Delaney, director of the Office of International Education at the University of Colorado, Boulder, agrees with Barr, Adams, and Sadler, emphasizing the importance of truly extending oneself to the faculty: "I think I have good working relations with the faculty members of my institution. I seek them out, ask their advice, try to assist them in matters of importance to them, and, most of all, respect them for their knowledge, skills, and dedication. I ask them to do worthwhile things for me, and I try not to bother them with trivia. I take them to lunch, visit them in their offices, write them memos, and, in general, try to be available to them when they call me or stop by my office."

John Koldus, vice-president for student services at Texas A & M University, agrees that seeking the faculty's advice is essential and has established formal mechanisms for doing so: "I have always had a faculty advisory committee, and I indicate that the members' input is important. We meet once a month during the academic year. We use faculty members on division committees and involve them in student-faculty luncheons throughout the year." Thomas Dutton of the University of California, Davis, also recommends "involving [the faculty] in the management of student affairs through service on advisory committees and other administrative bodies. This provides the opportunity for the student affairs staff and the faculty to have an ongoing dialogue about institutional and student needs and how these needs might best be addressed."

Larry Moneta, associate vice-provost for university life, University of Pennsylvania, makes the following observation about such advisory groups: "One successful [body] I've used has been a faculty advisory board. Such a body, meeting infrequently, provides a comfortable springboard to further interaction." Rosalind Andreas, vice-president for student affairs at the University of Vermont, notes how important this advice can be: "I have found faculty members to be most valuable resources. Faculty advice, from research interests and disciplinary perspectives, can be invaluable for us in our work." James Lyons, former dean of student affairs at Stanford University, also draws on faculty members in these ways but adds a different twist: "I always look for faculty members who have sons or daughters in college or about to go there. [They are] wonderful sources of support and service on committees."

In addition to seeking advice from faculty members, the leaders surveyed for this study see the importance of extending themselves as resources to the faculty. Rosalind Andreas relates, in the context of a previous position—dean of students at the University of Arizona: "I am very willing to attend departmental meetings and answer questions—face an inquisition, if need be—because I feel it is very important for the faculty to understand the multiple roles of a dean of students' office and the nature of students on the campus. I have always sought to be involved in new faculty training and in teaching assistant or graduate assistant training, and to have a description of the role that the dean of students' office can play to assist persons who will teach." This can be a two-way exchange, with student services professionals providing perspectives that the faculty may not have, and vice versa.

Michael Hoctor, director of housing and residential life at San Diego State University, talks about how important it is that faculty and staff members engage in dialogue: "It is important for us in student affairs to be active on our campuses with issues of concern to faculty members and to invite them to join us in discussions about those issues. For example, faculty members are concerned about student organizational behaviors, and they have insights to share with us; we can pursue these topics in the faculty centers, via invitation to faculty guest meal plans, faculty-in-residence programs, and so on. The main point is to keep in mind that we—faculty and student affairs staff members alike—have a stake in the education, in and out of class, of our students. We must continue to work at it, remembering that faculty members, too, have many pressures, which divert their attention from our issues of common concern."

Some leaders surveyed for this study identify roles for the faculty that extend far beyond advice. Rosalind Andreas seeks critical feedback. She relates, "I have had interesting experiences inviting a group of faculty members to critique the work of a unit. We have used a faculty community-standards group to critique how the judicial systems work with students in protecting and building an honest academic community. Looking at what we do, and discussing role differences for those who teach, advise, counsel, program, and discipline, has proven to be very helpful and has raised the level of dialogue across campus on the responsibility that each of us must take in a university community." It is noteworthy that Andreas has enough confidence in the worth of her units to invite faculty members to offer critical feedback.

Samuel Sadler of the College of William and Mary agrees that seeking critical feedback is important: "I have made it a habit to involve the faculty in a wide range of student affairs committees, task forces, and advisory groups, and I always place at least one faculty member on each of my staff evaluation committees. It has been especially helpful at times to invite faculty critics to serve on certain student life committees." It is interesting that these leaders do not fear critical feedback from the faculty. They seek it out as a means of establishing relationships and improving their functioning. This reflects confidence in themselves and in the collegial nature of their relationships with the faculty.

The leaders surveyed for this study offer other examples of ways to involve the faculty. One approach is to utilize faculty expertise. Arthur Sandeen, vice-president for student affairs at the University of Florida, suggests this when he urges that we "learn about faculty members as people and about their particular expertise. Then, by involving them in various activities on the campus that fit their skills and interests, we can often develop good relationships." The involvement of the faculty in such activities provides increased opportunities for "interaction, understanding, and appreciation" (Garland, 1985, p. 58). Margaret Barr of Texas Christian University suggests, "Look for ways that you can link up with the faculty through research, career planning, search committees, planning committees, and the like. Faculty members are no different from anyone else. They support what they help to create." Again, the idea of jointly shared responsibility is stressed.

James Lyons of Stanford talks about how research-oriented faculty members can be involved: "I generally try to enlist their services. Stanford has a powerful research faculty. Curiously, we also have more faculty members involved in our residential programs—thirty-nine as resident fellows, who live in but don't get paid—than any other university like us." Rosalind Andreas offers additional examples of roles that faculty members can play in student services programs: "I always try to encourage faculty involvement with students as club advisers, speakers, mentors, and participants with students in creating meaningful out-of-class experiences. At one institution, we started an academic cultural-events fund for that purpose." Larry Moneta agrees: "Faculty members are usually flattered by invitations from the student affairs staff to participate in serious interventions. These may include support for campus disciplinary boards, membership in task forces with limited but important agendas, and opportunities to offer critiques without obligation."

Michael Hoctor of San Diego State University brings

us full circle, back to the idea that the most effective faculty-staff relationships are built on respect for the academic mission of the institution: "Our department programs which improved our relationships with the vice-president for academic affairs are those which reinforce the university's academic purposes—faculty fellows, faculty-guest meal program, and so on. When we seek to involve the faculty in these or other programs, we obtain the vice-president's—and oftentimes the president's—cosponsorship. For example, we will have the president jointly invite faculty members to an event, and the vice-president signs all letters of appointment to the faculty fellow program." Hoctor's comments reflect his and other leaders' belief that the student affairs agenda supports the academic agenda of an institution of higher education.

There are many fine examples of collaborative efforts between faculty and staff members. Leaders note that if more such collaborations are to occur, the student affairs staff will have to take more initiative and be willing to share power and responsibility with the faculty. The result should be greater mutual appreciation and greater coherence in educational programs.

Joining the Faculty

Some leaders surveyed for this study advocate that the student affairs and academic affairs agendas be blended by having student affairs staff members establish their credentials as faculty members. James Quann, registrar and director of student information systems at the University of California, Santa Cruz, says, "First and foremost, in my opinion, student affairs people must be hired with and must maintain academic credentials similar to those of the faculty. We will not be totally accepted unless we are seen as equals. This may mean that, for top positions, we insist on the doctorate. It also means that we ought to have some teaching experience, if at all possible. If our staff members have the proper credentials, then I always recommend that we seek departmental affiliation within our disciplines and that we volunteer to teach, on occasion—one course per year is ideal. In this way, student affairs people will know better what is required of the faculty and what the faculty's expectations are. And, as colleagues, we will have better relationships and find that the faculty will be more willing to become involved in cocurricular affairs."

Daniel Walbolt, former vice-president for student affairs at the University of South Florida, concurs: "The key is to convince the faculty that student affairs staff members are equal partners in the learning process. The easiest way to do this is to have the student affairs staff teach courses, at least yearly, and participate in the affairs of the academic department in which the courses are taught." Brown (1972) advises that faculty-staff ties can be secured by having an academic department in which student development staff members teach classes in such things as human development, group skills, and human sexuality.

Alan Boyd, director of international student and faculty services at Ohio University, clearly articulates why teaching can be important: "Faculty members appreciate someone who sees the university as a teaching place and who understands the problems and pressures of the classroom, someone who does not come down on them from an administrative shelf, critical of them for lacking understanding of a student's problems." Thomas Myers, vice-president for student affairs at Eastern Kentucky University, agrees: "Most of our key student affairs administrators hold academic rank. Some teach a class, and all serve as guest lecturers. I believe faculty members see us as a partner, not as a threat."

If staff members are going to teach, some leaders say, it is important to legitimize their teaching credentials. Thomas Goodale, vice-president for student affairs at Virginia Polytechnic Institute and State University, recalls, "I have taught nearly every academic term since I have been in higher education. I have gained teaching positions through merit, not by any gift or handout. I served on academic committees and have gained academic tenure through the same route of promotion and tenure as my faculty colleagues." David McIntire, vice-chancellor for student affairs at the University of Missouri, Columbia, says, "We need to close ranks with our faculty colleagues—build bridges. If at all possible, we should teach one class every semester, publish, present, attend departmental meetings, seek tenure-track positions and rank. My appointment as a tenured full professor was not a ploy for job security, although that is a positive spinoff, but rather an acknowledgment of worth and accomplishment by faculty colleagues." Student affairs practitioners who become more "facultylike" by teaching and researching can enhance the credibility of the profession (Garland, 1985).

One leader surveyed for this study suggests a way to fully integrate teaching staff members. Thomas Magoon, director emeritus of the counseling center at the University of Maryland, College Park, recommends "fostering joint appointments whenever possible—either by split budgeting or by nonbudgeted affiliations."

Reflections on Leaders' Thoughts

Of all the topics covered in this study, relating to faculty members elicited the most divergent opinions. Some leaders believe that the obstacles are daunting. Others believe that meaningful relationships are possible if staff members show enough initiative. Still others believe that student affairs staff members will benefit from establishing academic credentials.

In a sense, this divergence of opinion is not surprising. The student services profession is composed of a diverse group of people, with differing levels of experience and different academic credentials, functioning at diverse institutions whose faculty members hold differing values and have different priorities. In that respect, the divergence of opinion makes sense.

Still, it would have been good to see more progress in more places on the issues of faculty-staff relationships. Brown (1972) calls attention to the bifurcation between student affairs and the traditional "academy" as an obstacle to the creation of a coherent program for student development. Fifteen years later, Boyer (1987) still sees fragmentation as characterizing undergraduate education in America.

One element of our slow progress on this issue may be the "guild" mentality of higher education. For Bowen and Schuster (1986), this mentality centers on the values of academic freedom, the search for new knowledge, and collegiality within faculty ranks. Over the last twenty years, ever since Brown's call (1972) for the faculty and staff to converge, the student affairs profession has increased its own similarity to a guild. With its stronger identity as a separate profession, its growing emphasis on specialized graduate education, and its increased attention to professional standards (Council for the Advancement of Standards, 1986) have come "separatist" incentives.

Some leaders surveyed for this study see the need for us to span both guilds. This could happen with increased contact and more meaningful involvement of faculty members in student affairs activities and of student affairs professionals in mainstay activities of the faculty.

The divergent opinions are understandable. The incremental gain is positive. Nevertheless, faculty-staff relationships continue to be an unmet challenge.

CHAPTER SEVEN

Working with Staff

The leaders surveyed for this study value their relationships with staff members and understand that their own success is inextricably bound to the success of their staff members. With that understanding, they pay great attention to hiring, empowering, team spirit, staff development, and thorough feedback.

Selecting Staff Members

Staff selection is a critical function that greatly influences the success or failure of student affairs programs and services (Rickard, 1984). The leaders surveyed for this study concur with that judgment. Leonard Goldberg, vice-president for student affairs at the University of Richmond, says, "Of all the decisions, probably the single most important that I must make is that of staff selection. People are our most important resource." William Brattain, assistant vice-president for student services at Western Illinois University, observes, "You are only as good as those people who surround you."

For the leaders surveyed here, a starting point in the hiring process is finding people with whom they are "in tune." John Koldus, vice-president for student services at Texas A & M University, says, "It's extremely important that you employ people with whom you are consistent philosophically and administratively. It's very difficult to motivate people who don't share your values." Tichy and DeVanna (1986) note that values can be an important screening device in hiring processes. Sherry Cook, former director of cooperative education at Southwest Missouri State University, strives "to find staff members who work well with my style. People I look for are already highly motivated and desire to do a good job because it's important to them—not just to me. So, first and foremost, I try to find people who need guidance—not motivation." Cliff Gillespie, dean of admissions, records, and information systems at Middle Tennessee State University, concurs: "I attempt to hire people who are aggressive, forward thinking, and able to mesh with my management style." James Osteen, director of Stamp Student Union at the University of Maryland, College Park, echoes this sentiment: "First, I try to hire self-starters who are motivated to perform at a high level, regardless of how I might supervise them."

John Schuh, associate vice-president for student affairs at Wichita State University, agrees that self-motivation is a key to effective staffing. He suggests, "Make sure that the people you hire are self-starters who are highly motivated. It is very difficult to motivate an unmotivated person. Threats, intimidation, pleas, and begging do not work with people who are not receptive." The contrast is obvious with motivated people. Eugene Seeloff, assistant dean for career planning and placement in the school of engineering at the University of Virginia, thinks that the key to motivating staff members "is selecting the right people in the first place. I have sought self-motivated achievers who have a strong desire or need to grow, to serve, and to help people learn what they need to know. If we do a good job in selection and hiring, people can more or less motivate themselves; all the leader has to do is orchestrate, provide lots of support, and not interfere or stifle them with too much supervision."

Kenneth Burda, vice-president for institutional advancement and former vice-president for student affairs of the State University of New York at New Paltz, describes an effective method of motivating staff members: "With the dramatic changes in funding for higher education and the subsequent tightening of the economy, motivating staff members has become even more critical. We have found that the opportunity to be promoted from within, which includes title changes and, many times, salary increases, is an important component of staff output. A study in the Office of the Vice-President for Student Affairs at the College at New Paltz has indicated that over seventeen semesters, sixty-five promotions had occurred, which carried $138,000 in salary increases for staff members. Remember that this was a very large and cumbersome system, where dollars had become more and more scarce."

Burda also offers a perspective on the importance of hiring a diverse staff: "We have developed an aggressive approach to searching for minority staff members and providing more than adequate training. Part of the reason is that we believe that successful staff relationships, as well as success within the minority staff, have contributed to a very healthy campus environment. The study I mentioned earlier also included hiring and promotion of forty-four minority people in the seventeen-semester period, and a 34 percent retention rate. Fourteen of the sixty-five promotions were for minority staff members."

Laurence Smith, vice-president for university marketing and student affairs at Eastern Michigan University, agrees with Burda: "I believe the key [to creating a positive climate for cultural and racial diversity] is to have an abundant number of culturally and racially diverse staff members who are also committed, with all others, to the goal of cultural and racial diversity and who see themselves as active agents in its attainment. We have been very open about our effort and our intentions. We have focused not on affirmative action but on affirmative results. Our institution and especially our division have come a long way, although we recognize that there is still a long way to go, to create a campus that has a positive climate for cultural and racial diversity."

Charles Frederiksen, director of residence at Iowa State University, shares the opinion that racial and cultural diversity of staff members promotes a positive campus environment: "I believe we must surround ourselves with a diverse staff reflective of our student body and learn how to promote real diversity from within. We learn best from day-to-day contact with persons different from ourselves, until we can begin to understand and actually appreciate the diversity of those around us."

The leaders surveyed for this study advise us to hire staff members who share our perspectives and values and are highly motivated. They highlight the importance of promoting from within, as well as hiring for diversity.

Empowering Staff Members

Several leaders surveyed for this study echo Eugene Seeloff's sentiment and talk about how self-motivated people perform when given the opportunity to assume responsibility. Raymond Heath, vice-president for student affairs at La Salle University, considers personnel selection and supervision "one of the chief student affairs officer's foremost responsibilities. In this particular setting, I have defined my role as being responsible for attracting the strongest individuals for a role they understand well in our particular context (urban, church-related, private, liberal arts) and hiring and developing the finest total staff possible, providing the resources they need, and then giving them the freedom and authority to do the work they love. From that point on, my role becomes consultative, depending on each director's differing capacity for independence." Kurt Zimmerman, director of placement and career services at the University of Toledo, outlines similar steps for motivating staff members: "Provide mutually agreed-upon goals and objectives; demand action plans and timetables; provide necessary resources; and reward performance on the basis of results." Heath and Zimmerman both feel strongly that staff motivation is a key responsibility and that when it is done well, leaders should have confidence that their staff people will perform well. Gardner (1990) also identifies this kind of motivation as one of the two tasks at the heart of effective leadership.

Valerie Woolston, director of international education services at the University of Maryland, College Park, agrees that staffing is vitally important. She talks about how she strives to maintain and retain an effective staff: "Probably the most difficult challenge that I've faced has been maintaining, training, and keeping excited good staff members in a very diverse office with, practically speaking, four very different professional divisions—admissions, advising, study abroad, and faculty services. I have tried to develop staff members so that they understand *why* they are doing certain things, instead of just training for *how* and *what*. Hopefully, we are also flexible enough to recognize when our *why* needs to change, and then it follows that the *how* also changes. I believe that when you give responsibility to a person to do any job, you must also give away authority, so that the person can successfully execute the task. This sometimes means mistakes are made, but it allows for immense growth, and chances are that the same mistake doesn't occur twice. I also try to instill respect for others' jobs within the office and will not allow one task or set of tasks to be viewed as less important than another or others. All the tasks are essential to the educational process of the student and to the institution."

Paul Pratt, dean of cooperative education at Northeastern University, says, "I am basically a nondirective manager, allowing those who report to me a maximum of independence in how they complete their assigned tasks. I establish basic and broad guidelines and interfere only when it is obvious that an individual is operating substantially outside the norm." Stanley Singer, former director of the counseling center at California State University, Northridge, agrees that freedom is a motivator for staff members: "Every professional staff member is free to develop whatever program or whatever interests he or she may have, as long as the prime consideration—taking care of students—is kept in mind. I have tried to respond to each suggested staff project with an attitude of 'Let's try to work this out.' "

Max Bromley, associate director of public safety at the University of South Florida, presents this idea in an interesting way. He says that to motivate staff, he provides "an environment where input is encouraged, then I give people the ball and let them run with it. I function as a resource and a coach, not necessarily as a boss." This approach can lead to a positive end, as noted by Roland Zick, former director of the Wardenburg Student Health Service at the University of Colorado, Boulder: "One of the most effective approaches that I have found is having the staff participate and giving the staff a feeling of ownership in the activities that affect the future of the student health service." Pratt, Singer, Bromley, and Zick have confidence that, within broad guidelines, staff members should be empowered to act independently.

Giving people the opportunity to assume responsibility is obviously important. Charles Nolan, dean of undergraduate admissions at Babson College, observes, "Allowing staff members to be the 'masters of their own destiny' in the context of a well-defined organization has been the single most effective stabilizer in building a committed team of professionals." Patrick Scheetz, assistant director of career development and placement services at Michigan State University, says, "A well-motivated staff is a confident, challenged staff. If personnel believe they have control of their own destinies, they are more likely to produce maximum results with minimum supervision." This approach has had positive results as well for William Rodgers, former director of financial aid at the University of South Alabama: "The most effective approach I have found to motivating staff members is to allow them to feel ownership in the process." Nolan, Scheetz, and Rodgers agree that empowering staff members motivates them.

Bruce Shutt, associate vice-president for student affairs and registrar at the University of Georgia, also talks about empowering strategies: "I have tried to give my staff members freedom with responsibility. I have attempted to gain their interest in new projects and new products by having them visit other institutions and attend professional organization meetings, seminars, and workshops and, from these, produce suggestions for change at this institution. I never say, 'That's been tried, and it won't work,' or 'That's old stuff, and we must go to something else.' In short, I've let them have freedom with responsibility in producing new and innovative systems at this institution."

Dalton (1989) also notes that opportunities for responsibility, growth, and achievement are powerful motivators. Freyda Lazarus, director of cooperative education at Montclair State College, confirms this: "I motivate staff members by including them in decision making, sharing information, delegating responsibility, and assuming that they will come through." Ruth Jass, former director of institutional research and registrar at Bradley University, says, "When I have built on strengths and on great expectations from my staff, when I have focused on contributions and on results, when I have listened to and rewarded my champions and risk takers, when I have shared plans and successes with my staff—then my people have risen to meet challenges and have even created some of these challenges, and they are happy in the process." The late Wayne Carlisle, as director of placement and career services at Wichita State University, used the same approach, and he advised, "Provide as much opportunity as possible for individuals to add new responsibilities and determine their own ways of accomplishing goals." There is a positive sense from Lazarus, Jass, and Carlisle that staff members, when given opportunities for inclusion, will do more than asked.

Of course, giving people autonomy does not mean distancing oneself. As Paul Pratt of Northeastern observes, "I have a total open-door policy and try to be available to advise and counsel on request. Generally, I try to lead by example. I have the mentality of a sheepherder: so long as folks are moving in approximately the right direction, I let them run, but I do nip at the heels of those who stray, and, if necessary, I thrash about in the brambles with those who are lost. To carry the analogy a bit farther, I also have been known to have an occasional leg of mutton."

The leaders surveyed for this study believe that staff members can be empowered through being delegated responsibility, being included in decision making, and being encouraged to take risks and define reasonable courses of action.

Individualizing Staff Development

Effective leaders recognize that they have a role to play in staff development. The importance of professional development has been highlighted by the Council for the Advancement of Standards (1986). In developing staff members, leaders respect their uniqueness and value their special talents and gifts. James Rhatigan, vice-president for student affairs and dean of students at Wichita State University, observes, "Students are not our only clientele. We should be wholly interested in the development of our staff members. Each of them has development goals, which we should support. Our role in contributing to the success of an individual staff member should be a point of pride." Leaders approach staff members with "a belief that each person is unique and of great value," in the words of Garold Tisue, director of the student resource center at San Diego State University. Timothy Sheridan, director of student judicial programs at Western Illinois University, expands on this idea: "Each member of one's staff brings special skills, interests, experience, and particular attractions to the office. A supervisor should recognize those qualities for each person, to determine how to meet individual needs."

By recognizing the individuality of their staff members, leaders can better assist them. William Bryan, vice-chancellor for student affairs at the University of North Carolina, Wilmington, asserts that "in motivating the staff, it is necessary to assess where staff members are in their own professional development, to know their competencies, and to help them enhance their skills in particular areas." Timothy Sheridan talks about contributing to the development of staff members:

"By providing appropriate challenges and supports, a supervisor can promote individual professional growth. Staff members need timely feedback regarding progress. Most new staff people require more initial direction and more immediate feedback. When difficulties occur, I encourage discovery of better alternatives through discussion. Gradually, as a staff member realizes more competence, I increase the amount of autonomy that person will have." Hersey and Blanchard (1988) characterize this style as situational leadership, whereby a leader diagnoses problems and applies the appropriate style, given the needs of the situation.

Michael Hoctor, director of housing and residential life at San Diego State University, recognizes the individual differences of his staff members and tells how these differences call for him to adjust: "I direct, coach, support, and delegate . . . ; establishing where the follower is, in terms of commitment and competence, and with respect to doing the specific work to be done, enables me to lead appropriately. Sometimes I have to give very clear instructions and continuous supervision; other times, lots of instruction and encouragement are necessary, or I provide a lot of support to an able but hesitant follower; still other times, I hand over the job to be done, with only a request to be kept informed."

This kind of individual investment is labor-intensive. William Klepper, dean of student life at Trenton State College, says, "I feel that I lead by being there and by example. I have always felt that the success of our program has resulted from the amount of time and personal commitment that was given to it." Thomas Carver, vice-president for student affairs at Berry College, believes that there is no substitute for time: "Nothing replaces personal time. Every person on the staff who reports directly to me has the opportunity to meet with me in a scheduled meeting for one hour a week. It is essential that the associate be completely tuned into every matter that I am dealing with." Joel Rudy, dean of students at Ohio University, agrees on the importance of committing time and energy to these relationships with staff members. He advises, "Get to know them, know what they think, know what they do, and try to express understanding and awareness. I also attempt to share expectations, both personal and professional."

This kind of time investment, coupled with placing a priority on staff development, has helped leaders capitalize on the contributions of their greatest resource—staff members. Thomas Flynn, vice-president for student affairs at Monroe Community College, says that he values a "staff development program which includes the opportunity to develop career ladders both in and out of the institution. I attempt to be intimately aware of the objectives and responsibilities of all staff members and to demonstrate to them, through appropriate interaction, that I care very much how successful they are in their jobs."

Leonard Goldberg of the University of Richmond is also supportive of this approach. He encourages "professional development through professional travel, on-campus workshops, visiting staff members in their offices, having individual lunches to explore how each one is feeling about the work environment, and listening to their suggestions for improving the university."

Since individualizing development is labor-intensive, leaders recognize the differences among staff members and adapt their own behavior to provide an appropriate blend of challenge and support. The result is staff development, important as an end in itself but also important to students and to the improvement of institutions of higher education.

Team Approach

In addition to focusing on individuals, effective leaders also give attention to the development of collective effort, drawing people into teams. William Bryan of the University of North Carolina explains, "In motivating staff, there needs to be a sense of a team and common commitment to a direction or mission in a division of student affairs. For there to be real motivation, I believe strongly that staff members must be involved in the development of ideas, challenged to identify possibilities which encourage their own growth."

Susie Ray, director of cooperative education at Western Carolina University, stresses the importance, in working with staff members, of a team approach. She advises, "Let them participate in the decision-making process. Let them know that we are all working as a team to accomplish our goals. When personnel feel that they are a part of the process, even though final decisions don't always go their way, they understand and continue to work with you." Frank Julian, former vice-president for student development at Murray State University, says, "As for my staff, we're a team. We plan together, get goals together, work on resource development together, evaluate each other and our programs, and celebrate successes together. I never make a major decision without soliciting their views and reactions to my ideas. We share a rich mutual trust and respect. They know I will support them, and they always support me. We treat each other as valuable resources to accomplish our jointly held goals." Donald Adams, vice-president for enrollment management and student life at Drake University, notes the outcome of this kind of team involvement: "There is mutual respect among all our staff members, which I find motivating and challenging."

Leaders recognize the importance of developing a team approach. This requires involving staff members in decision making, being certain that they share common goals, and progressing to a relationship of mutual respect.

Recognition, Feedback, and Evaluation

Effective leaders understand that people are motivated by feeling good about their performance. Marsha Duncan, vice-president for student affairs at Lehigh University, notes, "Anything that we do that instills pride in the staff, the division, or the university only strengthens the commitment and the fervor. We call it psychic salary, and I assure you that, in very different ways, it feels as good as monetary salary. Psychic salary doesn't provide any support for the mortgage, but it does support the heart and soul."

Effective leaders understand that staff members thrive

on this kind of recognition. William Weston, director of cooperative education at North Carolina State University, has experienced great success with a "positive approach, involving frequent expressions of appreciation to staff members for work well accomplished." Roger Morris, associate director of student development at the University of Oregon, says, "Staff members love to be told that they are doing a great job—that they are contributing and, because of their efforts, the activity is successful. I firmly believe in letting people know that they are doing a good job—writing them notes of appreciation, giving them little gifts to acknowledge events and/or holidays, making certificates for them, taking them to lunch or for coffee breaks, and telling them that I'm glad they are working for me."

Leaders recognize that these gestures of recognition matter. Joshua Kaplan, director of the student health services at Bowling Green State University, says that it is "most important" to let staff members know when they are doing a good job: "I think that everyone enjoys praise, especially from the boss." Robert LaLance, Jr., vice-president for student affairs at Middle Tennessee State University, says, "It is amazing how much mileage a leader can get out of a simple pat on the back in recognition of accomplishments that staff members have made. A phone call to commend a colleague on how well a problem was handled or how nicely a brochure was written will do wonders for keeping morale high, even in the absence of high salaries or other customary benefits."

In addition to recognition for their accomplishments, staff members need regular informal feedback. Francine Madrey, vice-president for student affairs at Johnson C. Smith University, advises, "It is important to let persons know on a continuing basis, not just annually, how well they are performing and what areas cause you, as supervisor, some concerns. The evaluation instrument and process can be intimidating, threatening, and counterproductive. Indeed, it is difficult for one to remember from year to year how well a subordinate has performed on a variety of dimensions. Frequent meetings and regular written assessments represent ways in which the supervisor may share with the staff various concerns, problems, and challenges, including suggestions that may assist employees' development."

David Butler, director of housing and residence life at the University of Delaware, maintains, "People need to know how they are doing as they go along. Even when you only have a gut feeling that things are not working right, share it with the person involved. Phrase it as a question, and let the person know that it is only a gut feeling. This lets your staff members know that you are straight with them in the beginning and gives them an opportunity to clarify what is going on that may be leading to your feelings. I am surprised at how many times the feelings have simply disappeared once we have talked it out."

Ronald Klepcyk, dean of student affairs at Elon College, says, "On a more informal note, positive reinforcement for hard work on a specific project is always helpful. I strive to find those things which are done well by the staff member and make a point of acknowledging such performance with that staff member, either verbally or in writing. Whenever possible, I also provide such positive reinforcement in group settings, where others will know how much I appreciate the staff member. While it is understood that there is a need for some sort of formal evaluation process, I can't emphasize enough the need to provide regular feedback on performance to staff members. To simply wait until the next formal evaluation period to provide feedback on performance will not be very helpful to the staff member. Positive reinforcement for job performance, provided on a regular basis, provides encouragement to the staff member, who then knows that his or her efforts are truly appreciated. This approach is also suggested for dealing with constructive criticism concerning job performance."

Continuous feedback can include dimensions that more formal annual evaluations do not. Francine Madrey of Johnson C. Smith University says, "The annual evaluation can be counterproductive in that the supervisor may be placed in the position of having to remember facts and details long since forgotten or may be challenged about the assessment process or outcome. More frequent assessments can help to ensure that certain issues, and their impact, are fresh in the minds of both parties, and that the supervisor is not viewed as using isolated incidents to measure overall performance. By shortening the period during which evaluation occurs, the supervisor helps to ensure the employee's growth and heightens the employee's confidence in and the integrity of the evaluation process. Moreover, the supervisor then has additional information to use in making personnel recommendations, awarding salary increases, and so on."

Many leaders also have strong views about the importance of evaluation as a motivator for staff members. They talk about how we give too little attention to this matter. Linda Kuk, vice-president for student affairs of the State University of New York, College at Cortland, observes, "The lack of sound and effective performance review programs is one of the more troubling dimensions of higher education organizations. Since our staff members are relatively independent practitioners, with limited resources and diverse responsibilities, feedback and evaluation are critical to their professional development, as well as to institutional effectiveness. Yet I continually hear horror stories of staff members who go for years without any type of effective performance feedback." Schuh and Carlisle (1991) identify good evaluation as vitally important for staff members who are pursuing careers in student affairs.

William Johnston, assistant vice-president for student affairs at Southern Methodist University, sheds some light on why people in the profession have difficulty with this issue: "We in higher education tend not to be effective evaluators. Because we deal in human development, rather than in the manufacture of widgets or the sale of material goods and services, we cannot define success in terms of productivity or profit. We can, however, provide *frequent,* insightful feedback, using mutually agreed-to criteria. Since 'cost of living' rather than honest-to-goodness 'merit' pay increases tend to be given, there is not the same direct tie between salary and evaluation in higher education as there is in the business world. There is a tendency to evaluate staff members as 'ideal' or 'above average' in order to maintain harmony and a sense of the team."

Some leaders believe that, by not evaluating staff members, we miss opportunities for constructive dialogue. This is certainly true when the appraisal system is constructive and developmentally based (Koontz and O'Donnell, 1972). Brown (1988b) also states that performance appraisal should be largely educational and developmental in orientation. Dorothy Pijan, director of the Thwing Center at Case Western Reserve University, notes, "I approach staff evaluation and performance review very positively. I welcome the opportunity to review the positive aspects of each member's performance over the year, to make him or her realize that he or she is an important member of the team that provides for the campus community. It also is an opportunity to look at areas in which improvements can be made and determine methods of improving that will fully utilize the person's potential." She goes on to say, "I see evaluation as a two-way process. The feelings and ideas of the staff member are very important to me, for they provide me yet another perspective from which to review the person. If there are weaknesses in performance, the staff member needs to be dealt with openly and honestly. Through such discussion, the staff member can participate in identifying the avenues that lead to improved performance."

Brown (1988b) notes that appraisal systems can focus on positive outcomes, such as recognizing good work, improving staff morale, and helping staff members improve professionally. To emphasize the positive nature that this process can assume, several leaders discuss how to set the tone. David Kratzer, director of the Reitz Union at the University of Florida, notes, "I look forward to periodic evaluation opportunities. Just about any evaluation system will work well if expectations are clearly defined prior to the evaluation period, and if the evaluation is tied directly to monetary rewards." John Bishop, dean of counseling and student development at the University of Delaware, says, "I believe that the time spent in staff evaluation is some of the most important of our administrative year. I approach it in a very formal and thorough manner. My goal is to provide each employee that I am responsible for with a rather detailed written evaluation of his or her work and to spend at least an hour with that employee, discussing my comments. My hope is that each employee will sense that I am well informed about his or her work, and it gives me an opportunity to provide as much positive feedback as possible to each individual. It also provides a forum for a formal discussion of any improvements in performance which I feel are needed. In short, the information and time given to a particular employee by a supervisor in evaluation of his or her work is one of the more memorable elements of any employee's work year. Supervisors who treat this activity in a cavalier manner are missing an opportunity to increase morale, shape behavior, and gain the respect of the employee."

Nancy Scott, vice-president for student affairs at the University of Northern Colorado, agrees with Bishop and shares the details of how such a constructive system might be designed: "We use a performance planning and evaluation system, which is intended to be developmental in nature and to promote a constructive exchange between supervisors and employees of the division. It consists of four phases. The first phase involves performance planning, which includes a description of the job responsibilities, the professional performance, the specific organizational objectives for which the person evaluated will be responsible, and the professional development goals of the person. This phase is conducted at the beginning of the academic year. The second phase requires a midyear review between the supervisor and the employee, which is an informal discussion of the performance plan and of any necessary alterations to the plan because of changing circumstances. This phase is conducted in December to January. The third phase includes a summary of the activities and accomplishments of the employee during the year. This is to be submitted to the supervisor in May of each year. The final phase includes a narrative description of the employee's performance and an evaluation of the professional performance, as well as of the success with which the employee has met the organizational goals and completed his or her plan for professional development." This type of complete process can serve as a basis for changing behavior to improve performance (Brown, 1988a).

In the design of such systems, it is important to involve the staff members who will be evaluated. Richard Artman, vice-president for student affairs at Nebraska Wesleyan University, explains, "In developing our staff evaluation and performance review process, we spent at least a full year, with staff input, on developing the criteria and format for the evaluation. What has evolved is a two-part format, which includes open-ended questions as well as a performance rating. Both the director and myself complete the form independently and then meet at year's end to review our relationship and performances from the past year and to plan goals for the next year. We also meet at midyear to assess our progress on goals for that academic year. Thorough preparation for these evaluation meetings is necessary, and providing specific feedback is essential."

Linda Mahan, vice-president for student affairs at the University of Montevallo, agrees. She advises, "With your staff, develop your own evaluation system. The staff's understanding and ownership of the system establishes confidence in its purposes and uses. Don't rely on annual evaluations alone; evaluate often, providing specific direction for desired improvements while giving praise for previous excellence in performance. Ask how you can help, and do so." This kind of involvement produces what Thomas Goodale, vice-president for student affairs at Virginia Polytechnic Institute and State University, calls "bonding and a willingness to share in decision making and to recognize both success and failure. Taking ownership in the total program produces a team effort, and everyone wins."

Despite constructive outcomes, evaluation of staff members who are performing below par can be difficult. Douglas McConkey, vice-president for student affairs at Ball State University, expresses the difficulty these situations present: "My most difficult challenge has been learning to effectively confront employees who are not performing up to the expected and required standard. Obviously, this could be due to laziness, poor attitude, basic lack of ability, mismatch between the individual and the position's requirements, or myriad other factors. The bottom line is that the individual is simply not contributing at the necessary level. I've learned to deal with this type of situation rather effectively, I believe, simply through practice. By confronting people openly and honestly, presenting the good news and the bad alike, I have found that individuals are either receptive and will change their behavior or will get the message and seek other employment. Rarely have I been forced to go very far down the 'due process' road—another acceptable solution normally develops. The point is that by practicing confrontation but also being supportive, I have learned that procrastinating does not help, and most times people appreciate the candor."

While many of the leaders surveyed for this study feel very positive about staff evaluation, some have less confidence in elaborate, formal systems. Raymond Heath of La Salle University talks about working with a structured system for three years and finally abandoning it: "Some of the merits of such an approach continue to be appealing, but, as a vice-president with as many as nine units reporting to me at one time or another, I prefer to rely on a thorough written annual report by each director, which serves as the basis for a meeting, often along with the president, during the summer, in which individual staff performance is discussed when there are problems which need attention. I now believe that the value of highly structured evaluation procedures is often exaggerated. Perhaps our different situation—no administrative contracts; all serve at the will of the president—influenced the many staff questions about the validity of the previous evaluation process, but I have not noticed a significant decline in performance since the required evaluation process was abandoned."

Some leaders have struggled to find a balance, viewing structured evaluations along a continuum. Harrison Morson, dean of student services at Mercer County Community College, says, "Like many of my colleagues, I find staff evaluation an anxious task. Personally, I have yet to find a standardized, prescribed performance chart or scale that proves to be satisfactory as a single indicator for a fair, reliable performance review. Standardized instruments may simplify the assessment of someone, however, after the first term of probationary employment. My preference is to use a narrative, with specific reliance on the management-by-objectives (MBO) model. With tenured, seasoned professionals, I encourage the MBO approach. It is more productive and certainly easier to monitor. Setting short-term goals and progress-review dates becomes essential," Morson advises. "Also, insist that each staff member identify what resources and support may be required from the chief student affairs officer. Strongly encourage staff members to pursue internships in areas of expressed interest, both on and off campus. Stress this option in contracted situations, where it would be virtually impossible to provide individual, direct benefits in terms of salary increases. Quite selfishly, I look for ways in which I can help staff members grow out of their present assignments, and I candidly tell them this, repeatedly."

The leaders surveyed for this study are realistic about how much they can do as supervisors. David Butler of the University of Delaware sums up this sentiment: "Above all, avoid becoming the person responsible for somebody else's learning and success. One of the biggest mistakes new supervisors make is to assume that if they 'do it right,' the other person's performance will improve, and they will have 'saved us all.' All you can do is provide direction and suggestions and an opportunity to talk them over. The bottom line is that the other person is responsible for his or her behavior, and no amount of work on your part can take that responsibility away. You have to try to help people learn and do better, and you have to take action when they fail to do so. No matter what you do, you cannot change other people. It is up to them."

It is evident that there are divergent opinions within this group of readers about the degree of structure to use in evaluation. Whatever forms or strategies are used, however, it is essential to provide staff members with thorough and thoughtful feedback.

Reflections on Leaders' Thoughts

The leaders surveyed for this study understand the importance of establishing strong relationships with staff members. They realize that they cannot be successful unless they create opportunities for the staff to be successful. Initially, this entails the selection of staff members who share the leaders' values and are self-starters. Leaders then find ways to empower staff members to take risks and act independently. Of great importance in building successful relationships is drawing staff members into effective teams, developing individualized plans for development, recognizing accomplishments, and providing feedback that helps staff members improve and develop their skills.

The leaders surveyed for this study are interdependent with their staff members. There is no sense of competition; a collaborative spirit creates a synergism that seems to benefit all parties.

Staffing is already complex and will become increasingly important as student populations continue to change. The value of hiring staff members who are "in tune" may compete with the value of hiring diverse staff members. The leaders surveyed for this study do not seem to see these values as being in conflict, but this certainly is an issue over which student affairs units will have to exercise vigilance. True recognition of diversity will have implications for hiring, developing, recognizing, and evaluating staff members.

PART THREE

Challenges That Test Our Capabilities

CHAPTER EIGHT

Managing Crises

Despite the traditional image of the calm "ivory tower" atmosphere, our college campuses are struggling with crises associated with a variety of issues, including environmental disaster, crime, natural death, policy conflicts, and international crises (Siegel, 1991). One of the essential challenges for the student affairs professional in the 1990s is to "assume leadership for the institution's responses to student crises" (National Association of Student Personnel Administrators, 1987, p. 16). Effective leaders in student affairs assume a variety of important roles in managing crises on their campuses. These roles are extremely important because such crises are perceived as campus problems (Siegel, 1991).

Leadership Roles

The leaders surveyed for this study work to avert crises but also accept their inevitability. As problem solvers, effective

leaders seize the "teachable moment" and act with the courage
of their convictions to turn crises into opportunities.

The effective leader's role begins before a crisis occurs.
Attempting to stay ahead of issues, Thomas Flynn, vice-president for student affairs at Monroe Community College, says,
"The best management is not to permit the crisis to occur. In
other words, identify situations that have that potential—be
preemptive rather than reactive."

Thomas Myers, vice-president for student affairs at
Eastern Kentucky University, reminds us that "individual
crises are not uncommon with a large student population."
Myers strives to keep ahead of the curve and has established
"a university committee to deal with individual crises, with
the objective of providing services needed and preventing
future, similar cases." One person on the committee serves as
media spokesperson. There is evidence that this kind of collegial leadership tends to be associated with positive outcomes
(Bensimon, Neumann, and Birnbaum, 1989).

John Koldus, vice-president for student services at Texas
A & M University, says, "We have problems of one kind or
another on a continuing basis. My contribution is that I have
worked hard over time to make myself visible, to interact in
an open, honest fashion, to be patient and reasonable, to be
open to ideas and change, to meet on a weekly basis with
student leaders, to be accessible to anyone who needs to see
me, and to support what's in the best interest of the students
and the university." Effective leaders maintain visibility, share
responsibility for crises with other members of the campus
community, and are organized in their presentations of the
campus and to the media.

Effective leaders also derive a sense of calm about these
matters from the realization that haste is not as imperative in
these situations as it may seem at first. Patricia Kearney, assistant vice-chancellor for student affairs at the University of
California, Davis, says, "I do not view events as crises. Very
early in my career, a doctor in the college health center told
me that he had practiced medicine for twenty-five years and
had only seen two real life-and-death situations, where a few

minutes made a difference. He believed it was important, in successfully responding to problems and issues, to have an attitude about the nature of problems and to understand that there is enough time to respond to them. I suppose that my greatest contribution when it comes to difficult events on my campus is bringing a sense of calmness and space to these events." Larry Moneta, associate vice-provost for university life at the University of Pennsylvania, expresses a similar thought, saying that "95 percent of what we declare to be crises are really not crises." This sense of calm helps leaders be effective when crises do arise.

Examples of Crises

The leaders surveyed for this study recounted crises that they have managed, and important principles have emerged. In general, the crises reported can be grouped into five major types: those involving threats from environmental conditions, those related to protests, those related to international conflicts, those related to campus policies and expectations, and those related to individual students.

Environmental Conditions

There are occasions when special conditions, such as the weather and accidents, precipitate a crisis. Incidents at Drake University, Washington State University, and Dickinson College provide three good examples.

Describing the management of a crisis related to an ice storm, Donald Adams, vice-president for enrollment management and student life at Drake University, recalls, "Since both the president and the provost were away from campus, I was the person responsible. It was interesting for me to review my behavior in this situation. I did the same things during an all-university crisis as I did when I was an RA [residence assistant]. When a serious incident occurred, I, as the RA, called the floor government together, and we held a discussion. We met later to share information and lay rumors to rest. During the ice storm, the first thing I did, as a vice-president, was make sure that the other vice-presidents and the deans clearly understood how we were going to make decisions. Next, we had a team of persons, who met at noon and late in the afternoon, bring everyone up-to-date on where we were with the crisis." As DePree (1989) notes, this kind of participative management guarantees that decisions will not be "arbitrary, secret, or closed to questioning" (p. 22). Adams's account continues: "The university engineer, architect, security officer, telecommunications personnel, and business manager—everyone who had some part in the university's physical plant—met and shared common information." Kouzes and Posner (1987) note that leaders are able to get extraordinary things done when they enlist the support and assistance of all who have a stake in a project or situation. Adams concludes, "I consulted with the president of the faculty senate, as well as the deans and other vice-presidents, regarding the closing of school and canceling of classes. I was personally involved in all meetings, and no distance existed between me and the people who were making decisions regarding the safety and security of the campus. Everything worked out well; electricity was restored to the campus after being out two evenings and the better part of three days." Adams emphasizes how important it is to pull together a strong crisis-management team that involves key personnel related to the particular crisis. He also notes the importance of staying in close contact with institutional officers and other campus leaders. Dressel (1981) emphasizes how important this kind of communication is by his observation that most crises result from failures in communication, when information is ignored, misinterpreted, or held back.

James Quann, registrar and director of student information systems at the University of California, Santa Cruz, employs many of the same principles outlined by Donald Adams. He explains how they applied during a natural disaster that affected Washington State University when he was a staff member there. He recalls, "On May 18, 1980, Mt. Saint Helens erupted, spewing several inches of volcanic dust all

over Eastern Washington. Washington State University was
in the fourteenth week of a sixteen-week semester. There were
conflicting reports and ideas about the hazards of breathing
the volcanic dust, and hundreds of students and their parents
demanded that they be allowed to go home without losing
credit for the spring term. Lengthy discussions were held with
a few key administrators and the council of deans, and the
registrar and two others were asked to draw up a plan to
allow those who wished to leave to do so without academic
penalty. I devised such a plan, calling for students who opted
to leave to do so and to receive either the grades they had
earned up to that time in each course, or a grade of "S"
(satisfactory) if it was not possible for a faculty member to
compute a more precise mark. Checkout procedures were put
in place, and over four thousand students successfully exited
the institution, with few problems." The key administrators
involved in these discussions were the deans and the registrar,
a combination that reflects the peculiar needs of the situation.
Quann pulled the right individuals together, acted decisively,
and helped students meet their academic and safety needs.

Leonard Goldberg, who is now vice-president of student affairs at the University of Richmond, describes the
Three Mile Island nuclear-plant accident of 1979 from the
perspective of his previous job as chief student affairs officer
at Dickinson College, about twenty-five miles from the power
plant. He recalls, "When the crisis erupted, most of our students were in the process of returning to campus, following
the semester break. Our switchboard was inundated with calls
from students and their families, inquiring about whether the
college would reopen or close down. Indeed, as one listened
to Walter Cronkite and his media colleagues, it was certain
that the world—or, at the very least, central Pennsylvania—
was in the process of melting down. In order to decide
whether or not our college should close, the president and
senior staff met continually with on-campus faculty experts,
as well as with off-campus governmental and other officials
and experts in nuclear energy. We needed accurate information to better understand the situation and alternatives. We

needed knowledgeable and objective sources of data in order
to combat the mass hysteria under way in the press and on
television.''

An important element in managing this crisis was to
draw on credible experts, who could provide reliable information. Going beyond the campus is helpful in some
situations.

Goldberg says, "After much deliberation and soul-
searching, we decided not to close down the school, although
formal classes were canceled. We determined that we were, in
fact, far enough from the site not to be in any immediate
danger. I was given the assignment of overseeing the twenty-
four-hour campus hotline, to receive incoming inquiries
regarding the college's decision to stay open. We explained to
callers that while classes were canceled, a full range of seminars, lectures, and related academic activities was being held
to help our students and the broader community understand
the nature of the crisis and the reactions to it." In a crisis,
managing information is important, and the use of a twenty-
four-hour hotline is an innovative approach.

Goldberg explains how the college took advantage of
this crisis as an educational opportunity: "Arrangements were
made for scientists, psychologists, sociologists, and numerous
others to contribute to our campus dialogue. We reinforced
the concept of civic responsibility and the role of the civil
defense authorities, the governor's office, and others to determine and communicate levels of risk. In sum, we grasped this
opportunity to turn a crisis into a 'teachable moment.' It was
a powerful learning and bonding experience for those who
chose to stay with us. Faculty members, administrators, and
students were committed to each other twenty-four hours a
day—in the classroom, in the dining hall, in the residence
halls—for the duration of the crisis. The campus became one
large coed fraternity, complete with our student-designed, silk-
screened T-shirts of courage, which proclaimed, 'I survived
Three Mile Island—I think!' The major disappointment in
this whole process was when the 'all clear' signal was communicated and the college was inundated with returning stu-

dents. We resumed normal operations, and the bond of our 'fraternity' rapidly deteriorated." Although a college would certainly not choose to confront such a crisis, effective leadership can help avert panic and provide an opportunity for education and the furthering of a sense of community.

These three environmental crises are all very different. One relates to a weather condition—an ice storm; another relates to an extreme natural phenomenon—the eruption of a volcano; the third involves a human error that altered conditions—an accident at a nuclear energy plant. Although these three crises were very different, the leaders involved in these situations employed some common principles. They remained calm and visible, demonstrating a sense of control. They drew on experts to educate themselves and give confidence to others. They shared leadership with key campus personnel and communicated with campus leaders and important external constituents. They acted decisively, with the best interests of students paramount, and each one used the crisis as a way to educate and to reinforce confidence in the campus.

Campus Protests

Student protests are a special form of crisis. They frequently involve conflict and place student affairs administrators in the sometimes conflicting roles of student advocate and institutional representative (Rickard, 1972).

Thomas Dutton, former vice-chancellor for student affairs at the University of California, Davis, relates an incident that occurred on his campus: "A group of students of color became very concerned about a number of issues related to diversity and perceived racism. The students initiated a noisy and angry demonstration in front of the administration building and presented demands to the chancellor. The demonstration was followed by an encampment and hunger strike in front of the administration building. Specifically, the students wanted quick resolution of alleged racism in the Spanish Department, creation of a cultural center, assignment of more people to Ethnic Studies, a commitment to institute an ethnic-studies requirement, and approval of a mural on a large exterior wall on the campus. The role that I played was to bring together key campus administrators, faculty members, and student leaders to define the problem and identify appropriate courses of action. Out of that consultation came an understanding that restraint was desirable while assessment and dialogue were under way. Through communication with the students over a seven-day period, we were able to gain a better understanding of their concerns and to identify possible administrative responses. My major task was to argue for calm and restraint while facilitating communication between campus decision makers and the students." Here again, calm and visible leadership was important, as was pulling together the key members of the campus community.

"After a very difficult and tense week," Dutton says, "an agreement was reached, and the hunger strike ended. Simply put, I would describe my contribution as facilitation, assessment, communication, and identification of appropriate administrative responses." Dutton's example highlights the importance, in such crises, of helping students identify appropriate responses. A protest may result from misunderstanding of alternatives or from frustration with available alternatives. Clarity can guide the identification of solutions.

Dutton says, "Although there were some minor violations of policy and some suggestions that force be used, I feel that the process of consultation made it possible for us to get though a very tense situation without arrests and harm to long-term working relationships." There is a recognition here that the short-term goal of establishing order may affect the long-term goal of establishing good relationships. This is obviously an important element in managing campus protests.

Thomas Goodale, vice-president for student affairs at Virginia Polytechnic Institute and State University, describes his role in managing reactions to a Ku Klux Klan march in Blacksburg on January 20, 1991: "What could have been a very ugly and distasteful incident brought together a coalition of community persons, students, faculty, and staff to essentially 'boycott' the Klan march [to avoid according it credibility and to prevent confrontations]. Through networking with a number of individuals throughout our community, through using the trust that had been nurtured and built with students and faculty, we joined together and planned for six weeks for this very difficult event. The institution truly developed a sense of community through this crisis, and while the outcome wasn't perfect, we averted major problems, to say the least." This situation demonstrates how one can turn a crisis into an opportunity.

Stuart Sharkey, vice-president for student affairs at the University of Delaware, observes, "One of the most difficult dilemmas we face is the issue of divestment [of the institution's resources in South Africa]. If you believe in divestment and the board's policy is not to divest, you are obliged to uphold the board's policy. In terms of what you do about it, you participate in discussions at the higher levels of administration regarding divestment. In addition, you can assist student groups that are concerned about the divestment issue in conducting appropriate activities. For example, a rally was being held, and we worked closely with the faculty and students to ensure that the rally met university policy guidelines. In fact, the university facilitated the rally by removing obstacles that were in the way." Sharkey clearly sees the conflict between being an institutional administrator and being an advocate for students. He explains that effective leaders must accept their administrative role but must also help students voice their concerns and find reasonable outlets for protest. This attitude reflects Gardner's statement (1990) that the purposes of a group are well served when a leader helps members develop initiatives, use judgment, and, through this process, enhance their own growth and development. The actions of Sharkey and other leaders surveyed for this study reflect this conviction about handling student protests.

Thomas Dutton of the University of California, Davis, also comments on this issue: "A few years ago, students pressured colleges and universities to fight racism in South Africa through divestment. Our campus had a major conflict over this issue. Students engaged in a twenty-eight-day camp-in on the front steps of [the administration building]. Although the campsite was an irritant, we were able to maintain access to the building, and the students were generally cooperative. One group of students, however, decided to occupy the chancellor's office. The dilemma I faced was that I was sympathetic with their goal of achieving divestment and thereby putting pressure on the South African government to eliminate apartheid; on the other hand, as an officer of the university, I had the obligation to maintain the integrity of university policy and regulations. I decided to assume my responsibilities as an administrator. The students were informed that they would be arrested if the occupation continued, and after an appropriate waiting period, about twenty students were arrested. Later, many students requested that the charges be dropped because their cause was right, and nothing could be gained by prosecution. Again, I was sympathetic with their cause but felt obligated to observe the university policy that once an arrest has occurred, the matter is in the hands of the district attorney, and the campus will not intervene. I felt that it was important as well to support the position that civil disobedience has consequences, and to set aside the arrests would be inconsistent with the philosophy of nonviolent protest." These difficult decisions represent choices among important values—the freedom to protest, the freedom to live in a safe environment, and adherence to order, rules, and even the law. Dutton's perspective is important to note: he supports the right to protest, but he thinks that students should be held accountable for their actions by realizing the consequences.

One key element of successfully managing protests is having staff members who empathize with the student protesters. Thomas Magoon, director emeritus of the counseling center at the University of Maryland, College Park, recalls, "During the activism era, the counseling center's staff ordered considerable understanding and support of campus dissenters, when there were relatively few doors open to them. One of the most useful guidelines that I stumbled on was to ask myself how a dispassionate observer would judge the alternative positions we might take. This guideline has served me well." Magoon's comments reflect the roles of student affairs personnel as counselors, advisers, and educators.

Another key element is access to facilities. William Brattain, assistant vice-president for student services at Western Illinois University, discusses the importance of maintaining opportunities for freedom of expression. Recalling a previous position, he says, "I was a staff member at Indiana during the turbulence of the late 1960s and early 1970s. We tried very hard to make the union a place where debate and discussion could take place. This meant we argued strongly for keeping the building open all night during a few crisis situations and not trying to evict students at closing time. This contributed to the students' feeling that the union was their building, and it was never taken over. The Indiana Memorial Union has an extensive art collection, and none of this was damaged." The operating principle here is to provide facilities where debate can take place, so that students have constructive outlets.

Effective leaders realize that college campuses will be sites of discussion, debate, and sometimes conflict. These are inevitable in educational environments that encourage exploration, risk taking, and the development of values and civic responsibility. In fact, Miser (1988) projects that the 1990s will bring intense periods of activism around a variety of issues (for example, divestment, treatment of AIDS, environmental concerns, and gay and lesbian rights). Leaders can be effective as counselors and advisers to students, particularly when they empathize with students' concerns. Leaders can also provide facilities where students can safely hold debates, and, when protests occur, they can assist students in planning safe and constructive demonstrations. Underlying all the leaders' comments is the belief that the role of the effective student affairs practitioner is not to prevent debate or protest but to facilitate them and ensure that the students and the institution are well served by them.

International Conflicts

Over the last several years, conflicts abroad have triggered crises on campuses in this country. In particular, conflicts in Iran, China, and Kuwait have caused campus administrators to recognize how much the global community affects our campuses.

Gary Althen, foreign student adviser at the University of Iowa, expresses the impact that such incidents can have on a campus: "One major crisis in the foreign student field in the last decade had to do with students from Iran. Another involved students and scholars from the People's Republic of China. It seems possible to draw some instructive generalizations from responses to those two crises. The Iranian crisis came when militant Iranian students took over the American embassy in Tehran. At the time of that event, there were large numbers of Iranian students in the United States. They suffered in many ways, during and after. Money stopped coming from home. Their government was slow or inactive in keeping them informed about what was happening in their own country. They lost contact, for some periods of time, with their families. Many were advised by their families at home not to return, because conditions there were so bad. Thus, the students' life and career plans had to be tossed aside. Finally, the reactions of the American communities where the Iranians lived were often less than welcoming."

Althen goes on: "The Chinese crisis came as a result of the Tiananmen Square events in the summer of 1989. Unlike the Iranian students in the U.S. at the time of the crisis in their country, the Chinese got sympathetic responses from the Americans among whom they lived. Nevertheless, their future lives were drastically altered by the violent antidemocratic incident in their own country. Many, if not most, decided as a result of Tiananmen Square that they would have to revise any plan to return to their own country.

"In both crises, foreign student offices were called on to do similar things. First, they had to get information from appropriate official sources, including the United States gov-

ernment and the governments of the other countries concerned, and disseminate that information to the right people.
During these crises, foreign student offices were looked to as
natural intermediaries between the foreign students and scholars who were affected and the institutions that surrounded
them here.

"Next, foreign student offices had to remain in contact
with the students and scholars in whose countries these developments were taking place. We had to let the students and
scholars know that we were concerned for their welfare and
that we were doing everything we could to obtain information for them when they were suffering so much from ambiguity and uncertainty about what was happening and what
its implications were.

"In addition to keeping foreign students and scholars
informed, we had to keep our own higher-ups informed of
the legal developments concerning the students and scholars
affected and of the implications for the students and scholars,
both immediate and longer term. Higher-ups in the administration relied on foreign student offices to be knowledgeable
about legal and technical developments and to be in touch
with the students and scholars affected by the crisis. If a foreign student office was not performing well in either of these
roles, it could not expect to have the respect or support of the
higher administration.

"A final task that fell to foreign student offices was that
of informing the public about the group concerned. Crises
bring considerable media attention, and, in crises affecting
groups of foreign students and scholars, the media turn to
foreign student offices for knowledgeable opinions and cogent
perspectives on whatever the issues are. A foreign student
office that is in a position to respond quickly and knowledge-
ably to these requests stood to gain stature in the eyes of the
public and of the higher levels of the administration."

Alan Boyd, director of international student and faculty
services at Ohio University, offers another perspective: "The
war in Iraq and Kuwait put a great deal of pressure on students from those countries, as well as on students from coun-

tries affected by the loss of trade and by the human tragedies caused by the war. With our guidance, the university made available emergency enrollment possibilities for the students affected, provided funds for personal expenses, and supported the morale of the students. We have tried hard to help the university understand that international students bring the world to us, in both positive and negative ways. We encourage everyone to understand what is happening, to participate in responding to the students' needs, and to learn from them." William Brattain of Western Illinois University concurs, and he notes the educational role that the student union can play: "We need to try to provide an arena in which debate and discussion can take place, to try and keep this separate from our own personal feelings about U.S. involvement in [a particular] region."

Effective leaders recognize that international conflict can precipitate campus crises, and that we have an emerging global community. They realize that they have responsibilities to the international students most directly affected by these conflicts, as well as responsibilities to inform, educate, and legally protect the larger college or university community.

Policies and Expectations

Campuses have a variety of constituents whose needs do not always mesh comfortably. Given the expectations that these constituents have of higher education, the resulting pressure can precipitate crises. Dressel (1981) believes that crises have different meanings for different people, given the importance of the different issues at hand or the values held dear. The leaders surveyed for this study reflect the same belief as they talk about a variety of conflicts. Three crises concerning standards of behavior and underlying values are illustrative.

Judith Chambers, vice-president for student life at the University of the Pacific, recalls the campus tenor of the late 1960s and early 1970s as one of excessive liberalism that could lead to chaos: "During those years, under considerable pressure from the students and from the faculty, we dropped many of the academic standards we had previously held to. We did not lower admissions standards, but we took students who were 'different.' We gave academic credit for independent study that would never be approved today. We accepted behavior from students who operated on the theory of 'if it feels good, do it.' We seemed to have dropped all standards of conduct, and virtually any kind of behavior became acceptable because we were trying to 'understand the times' to death! During this period, I found myself and other staff members spending countless hours and exerting intense emotional energy defending students' rights with other students, providing counsel and support to students and faculty members, attempting to squelch rumors and keep behavior from erupting into violence, and trying to move the campus, through dialogue and education, toward a new level of understanding, tolerance, and acceptance.''

Baxter Magolda and Magolda (1988) emphasize how helpful it can be in such conflicts for administrators to debate issues directly with protesters. Chambers also stresses the important role that student affairs personnel can play in such crises. This role entails engaging students, faculty members, and staff members in productive and sometimes conflict-ridden dialogue and facilitating a process that elevates the community's understanding of the issues at the heart of conflicts. Chambers alludes to a kind of leadership characterized by Burns (1978) as transformational and fostering outcomes of mutual stimulation and elevation for leaders and everyone else involved. Chambers feels that such leadership will be necessary as campuses face the challenges of the future: "My greatest fear is that we have only witnessed the beginning of this struggle. My greatest hope is that we will be able to muster the resources and energy for diversity to thrive and grow on our campus." She cites the energy and commitment that effective leaders will need as we continue to broaden the scope of the students whom higher education serves.

A second type of issue that frequently confronts campus leaders has to do with "town/gown" relationships and expectations of students' behavior. Tom Thielen, vice-president for student affairs at Iowa State University, explains, "Important community leaders were very vocal and critical of the university's response to alcohol- and substance-abuse issues in the student body. My role was to counter the criticism in public forums—for example, written and visual media, speeches, and so on—in such a way as to acknowledge the problem but question the accusatory behavior and request the entire community to work together on this issue. We have expanded and improved our university educational and intervention programs and have made meaningful links with community efforts in substance abuse. What started as an adversarial relationship has turned to a partnership effort." Thielen's remarks highlight the importance, in such crises, of educating one's constituents and appropriately challenging 'wrong" thinking while working to enlist the cooperation of those who challenge us. There is a sense that everyone wins when a viable solution is identified through cooperative effort.

A third situation related to behavioral expectations is described by Gary Pavela, director of judicial programs at the University of Maryland, College Park, who recalls the problems and pressures that followed the death of basketball star Len Bias: "Maryland drug policies were subject to scrutiny after Bias's death. There were immediate calls for very strict penalties, including automatic suspension for any user of any prohibited drug, even for a first offense. In the midst of all the negative publicity and pressure from local and national politicians, we were faced with the immediate issue of what sanctions to impose on other students who were found to have used cocaine around the time of Bias's death. My office supported some increase in our standard sanction for use of drugs—we had always expelled dealers—but I was unwilling to apply the new sanctions retroactively. Our public relations people were very uneasy.

"There is no doubt that many observers were expecting suspensions or expulsions for the first-time offenders involved. We disappointed them, and they expressed their disappointment. From the vice-president for student affairs we received support for our decision that was critical and allowed us to maintain the fundamental integrity of our disciplinary system. We now have very strict penalties for drug users and require even first-time offenders to submit to ongoing drug testing or be suspended. But these penalties are imposed after proper notice to students, and after a major educational program designed to inform them about the reasons for our policy."

This situation clearly illustrates the public relations problems that surround such a crisis. Everyone involved was concerned about students' safety and appropriate sanctions for students who used drugs, but Pavela needed to assert the importance of another value: that of due process and protection of the university's relationship with students. Retroactively changing the sanctions would have pleased some constituents, but students' rights might have been compromised, and the university's relationship of trust with the students might have been put at risk.

All three of these dilemmas could have led to major crises but did not. As the leaders surveyed for this study can attest, values, determination, and hard work are tools for averting more serious crises.

Individual Students

The leaders surveyed for this study shared poignant examples of crises related to individuals that had the potential to trigger even greater ones. In handling these crises they demonstrate both advocacy for the individual and concern for the community.

Charles Schroeder, former vice-president for student development at Saint Louis University, describes the actions he took at that campus when a female student reported that she had been raped on campus at 1:00 P.M. on Labor Day: "The circumstances of the rape were quite frightening—she was abducted on a walkway, carried to a van, tied up, and raped in the van. Naturally, this report created considerable anxiety among our students, particularly female students. I immediately created a crisis-management team that dealt with the situation from multiple perspectives—health, safety, public relations, and so on. We distributed written updates to all students on campus on a regular basis. In addition, we convened a town meeting to bring students up-to-date on the status of the investigation. Our aggressive, open, and honest response was viewed favorably by students, the faculty, and the staff, as well as by external constituents. Again, our success in this crisis was based on an assertive, proactive response." While this kind of incident could cast an institution in a negative light, as unsafe, Schroeder shuns this concern and favors informing the larger community and creating an atmosphere of trust in the institution and its leaders.

Edward Webb, vice-president for student affairs at Humboldt State University, shares the tragic story of the murder of a graduate student a few years ago: "Her body was found in the community forest behind the university, in an area that our students used regularly to hike, bike, and stroll in. At the same time, a serial rapist was at large in the community, and two of our students were victims of these assaults. What I try to remember in such crises is to take advantage of 'the teachable moment.' There was much to be done in terms of calming fears, teaching safety and caution, mourning the death of a popular student, and coming together as a community. There was the inevitable 'open mike' that is always a healthy outlet for feelings. There was a candlelight march and vigil. There were workshops on personal safety and the resurrection of an escort service. Mostly, it was a matter of coordinating and publicizing the energy of many diverse groups. It's always amazing to me how students, faculty members, and staff people come forward in these crises; our job is to make certain that leadership for this energy is provided.

"Fortunately, the rapist was caught and convicted, and the body of the demented murderer, a former student, was found; he had killed himself. Gradually the crisis abated, but the feeling of community that had been established persisted for the remainder of the year." Webb speaks eloquently here about the importance of keeping the community informed, providing opportunities for students to express themselves,

encouraging service units to support activities, and using catastrophic events to reaffirm commitment to community.

Edward Blankenship, executive vice-president and director of the college division at the American Institute for Foreign Study, recalls a death that occurred at the California
State University, Long Beach, campus, when he worked with
international students there: "Probably the most difficult challenge which I have ever had to face was dealing with the
death of a foreign student. I had worked in student development for several years before I encountered this experience,
and I found that I was not prepared, in many ways. I had no
idea what this would involve, including dealing with the
bureaucracies of my institution, a foreign government, an
airline, a hospital, a funeral home, and, most of all, the student's family. The logistical and financial complications were
dramatic, especially given the fact that the student did not
carry insurance. I consulted several colleagues for advice and
guidance and, by drawing several key staff members together,
was able to handle the situation. As a result of this experience,
our institution has a mandatory insurance requirement which
has an expatriation clause. I strongly advise every institution
which has international students to have such a requirement." Blankenship's comments reflect an understanding of
the complexity that such situations involve, particularly with
international students, and he illustrates how effective leaders
learn from difficult situations and develop ways to improve
institutional policy and practice.

Reflections on Leaders' Thoughts

The leaders surveyed for this study accept crises as natural
outgrowths of human development in a community setting.
They see the student affairs professional's role as vital, and
they assert leadership in managing crises.

Important crisis-management principles emerge from
these individual cases. When a crisis occurs, effective leaders
ensure that they are fully informed about the situation, and
they call on experts, as necessary. They share responsibility

with others on campus, pulling key people together for the purposes of sharing information, seeking input, and making decisions. Communication, by whatever means, is an essential element of crisis management. Effective leaders remain visible and act decisively, with firm values, a view of long-term consequences, and commitment to individuals, to the community, and to the educational process.

As these leaders describe their experiences in managing crises, one gets a sense that they relish their roles. They seem to jump into the middle of whatever crisis is at hand and define viable leadership roles for themselves. It may be that this helping role comes easily to these leaders because so many of their day-to-day responsibilities involve problem solving; after all, they chose their profession because its demands satisfy their own personal need to help others. Crises give leaders the opportunity to assume a role that is natural to them—one with which they have experience, and one that fulfills their own need to assist others—on a larger scale, and in more demanding circumstances.

CHAPTER NINE

Coping with the Demands of Day-to-Day Practice

In considering which issues present challenges, the leaders surveyed for this study point out day-to-day dilemmas. They name issues involving diversity, confidentiality, favoritism, resources, and managing time and multiple demands.

Diversity

The changing nature of the student population on many college campuses is a challenge to college administrators, at all types of institutions and at all levels. James Lyons, dean emeritus of student affairs at Stanford University, identifies racial issues as a key challenge: "For my first fifteen years of being a chief student affairs officer, the challenges were to attract and retain greater numbers of minority students. That, in retrospect, turned out to be the easier task. That focused on the students themselves. The tough job now is tuning the institutional environment (and all that that implies) so that minority students feel fully welcome members of the community—to move to a point where their comfort levels are no different than those of all students. The challenges here are too numerous to discuss. Said simply, the hardest part of our work in these areas is just beginning; it will be a significant part of our professional agenda for at least one full student affairs generation and probably even longer." Indeed, Fleming (1984) notes that today most African American students are enrolled in predominantly white institutions, and she observes that the challenge for them will be to thrive in these environments.

Linda Kuk, vice-president for student affairs of the State University of New York, College at Cortland, shares this perspective: "As I wrestle with the question of diversity and difference among and between students, I am continually struck by the sheer complexity of the concept and the issues that surround it. Our institutions have become multicultural communities, where the facets and character of difference play out their dramas in the course of day-to-day interaction. Like many of our colleagues who serve as chief student affairs officers, I was thrust into a role bearing considerable responsibility for orchestrating the formation of this 'new' campus community, with little preparation or warning. Building on the pain and surprise of trial and error, I have come to realize that most of our old paradigms and models just don't work.

"I have also come to believe that we have been guilty of two critical errors in the development and application of student development theory. Some of this error was due to the pragmatic reality of limited resources and demographics; but, despite the reasons for its existence, the resulting state of affairs has added to the current complexity and volatility of our campus environments. Initially we attempted to think of all students as 'alike,' homogenizing our theory and practice to comport with models that reflected a singular, linear understanding of human development. More recently, we have attempted to correct this error by clustering students within various ethnic, gender, and/or organizational subgroups, creating a singular 'cultural' dimension for defining the notion of 'alike' (for example, African American students, Greek students, women students, gay students, athletes, Jewish students, and so on). This tendency to lump students into unidimensional clusters and categories has clouded our ability to see and address the unique differences among and between students and to effectively address the multifaceted developmental and educational needs that each of them presents. To our surprise, there is often as much diversity within a group as there is between groups, and at the same time there is often more commonality within diversity than initially perceived. We now need to move beyond limited, simplistic, and oftentimes polarizing approaches to identify development and advance more sophisticated, interactive models for understanding human dynamics. The real challenge before us is to build new models that balance the competing needs of difference within the context of the multifaceted dimensions of our human makeup, with the tasks of establishing a commitment to common educational goals and cross-cultural social responsibilities. With our dwindling global system, a community is no longer a nicety—it is a necessity." Kuk eloquently expresses the urgency that this issue engenders. Smith (1989) too notes that successful involvement of diverse populations in higher education today has implications for higher education and for society at large.

Ronald Beer, vice-president for student services at Oklahoma State University, also discusses the challenge of racial and cultural diversity and describes an approach that works on his campus: "The challenge to create a positive climate for cultural and racial diversity on campus is enormous but essential. We must create dialogue among the various ethnic populations (and especially with Caucasians) and persist in sharing concerns, problems, ideas, and solutions so as to better understand the diversity of backgrounds and the rationale for our beliefs and customs and acknowledge that it is okay to be different. We have implemented a multicultural action team composed of students (some of whom must represent minority populations), faculty members, and administrators (representatives who must come—deans and vice-presidents—to ensure proper connections at upper levels). Among the many tasks are creating greater awareness of and sensitivity to the diversity of cultures on our campus, investigating accusations of racism, stimulating culturally diverse programming throughout all areas of the institution, and constructively and positively confronting those who are insensitive to cultural diversity. Faculty and staff members, along with trained student leaders, must persist year-in and year-out in the tasks of helping the larger population to be more sensitive to and understanding of our diversity."

David Butler, director of housing and residence life at the University of Delaware, talks about how we need to move beyond traditional approaches: "Students have been giving us clues for years that there is a need for something beyond training and programming. They have told us that they are uncomfortable on our campuses and that devaluing messages are common in our environments. In an attempt to discover the meaning of these clues and to develop a more comprehensive approach to diversity, the Office of Housing and Residence Life at the University of Delaware engaged in a yearlong self-study designed to bring the department's total functioning in line with the diversity vision established for itself.

"In the midst of this experience, it appears to me that training and programming are far too simple a solution to a complex reality. Getting at the heart of our organization, in relationship to its impact on diverse populations, may be more painful and time-consuming but may lead to concrete changes necessary for the creation of a climate that meets the needs of an increasingly diverse student population."

These leaders accept Green's idea (1989) that a pluralistic campus will improve the quality of life for everyone. Their understanding of these complex issues reflects true commitment to creating a campus environment that appreciates differences. Their actions reflect the resolve to move this agenda forward.

Confidentiality

One issue that presents important challenges to the leaders surveyed for this study is confidentiality, or sharing of information. This issue has received attention in the statements of ethical conduct of professional associations for student affairs practice (Winston, 1989).

James Rauker, vice-president for students affairs at Worcester State College, says, "There are many difficult ethical issues that develop in student affairs, but probably the most difficult and continuing problem has to do with the sharing of information. Many pieces of legislation limit access to and sharing of information with other people, including members of the family. The issue has to do with how one effectively protects confidentiality and at the same time attempts to inform the appropriate people. Most cases develop around suicide attempts, drug use, mental health problems, and different types of judicial actions. The most difficult situation for me involved a student's alleged suicide attempt and the need to inform the student's parents. Fortunately, as in most other cases, we were able to prevail upon the student to agree to share the information with the parents." Rauker affirms the importance of maintaining confidentiality, but he also encourages students to make appropriate disclosures.

Issues that "demand judgments on balancing the autonomy of individual students and the expectations of parents regarding their welfare" have constituted the most frequent ethical dilemmas for Richard Artman, vice-president for student affairs at Nebraska Wesleyan University: "At what point do we inform parents of chemical dependency, eating disorders, or emotional instability, without the student's consent? The most frequent type of ethical dilemma I have faced deals with matters that are shared with me, in confidence, by staff members, and that affect the immediate and long-term interests of the university. An example would be an instance of sexual harassment to which there is no witness willing to step forward and make the accusation." Artman emphasizes that these dilemmas can be heartrending and life-threatening.

Issues of confidentiality also involve the law, as Thomas Carver, vice-president for student affairs and dean of students at Berry College, relates: "Although this particular incident is not the most difficult ethical issue I have faced, it is a good demonstration of how legal maximums are only moral minimums. On the day a young woman was to be suspended for the use of illegal drugs on the campus, her father coincidentally called me about some concerns he had about her. She had never signed the proper forms giving permission to relay any information to her parents, and when her father called and asked for various details about how she was progressing, it became painfully clear that I had to decide whether to inform him that she was being suspended that day. I chose to tell the father that she was being suspended, and what she was being suspended for. Later, the young woman secured an attorney, who wrote to the Department of Education. The upshot of the matter was that I was censured by the Department of Education for violation of the Family Rights and Privacy Act. If this kind of thing were to take place tomorrow, I would do exactly the same thing, the reason being that I felt it was the ethical thing to do, and legal maximums in most cases are only moral minimums." The issue of confidentiality is the legal and ethical issue most frequently discussed in counseling services (Yarris, 1988).

Carver's example, together with those presented by Richard Artman and James Rauker, illustrates how serious and wrenching struggles about confidentiality can be. As this situation illustrates, professionals sometimes have to confront choices that involve reasoning based on principles and the requirements of law. Leaders understand the law and respect individual rights but also apply their own values and their professional values to issues of confidentiality and student welfare.

Favoritism

Since the leaders surveyed for this study are involved in dispensing services to others, it is probably inevitable that people will implore them to do favors, which may entail the exchange of information, the award of access to someone undeserving, or the accommodation of a person of influence. Leaders struggle with these issues, as the following examples indicate.

James Grimm, director of housing at the University of Florida, names requests from "friends of the university" as a difficult and constant issue faced by housing professionals: "Administrators, deans, and presidents use housing as a means of granting favors. I have found two ways in which to handle this dilemma. One is to explain to your supervisor your ethical standard relating to this situation and ask that he or she handle those matters and, when the decision is to offer a facility, that it come as a directive from him or her. The second way, which is more difficult, is to react to the situation directly by ensuring that all the facts and results of such action are completely known to the individual who is making the request. In this manner, you are shifting the burden of the decision to the person making the request. It is also essential, in explaining these facts, that you ensure that the person knows your decision is negative. It is very important to hold the line in this particular approach." Grimm adds, "There well could be a situation where the appropriate authority does have a better opportunity to view a situation than the director of housing. It is important to maintain the integrity of your position and the integrity of your department, but it is also important that you maintain respect and understanding of the larger picture of the institution." Grimm notes the importance of being clear with supervisors about such matters, as well as being clear about one's thinking with the people who make such requests.

For Michael Hoctor, director of housing and residential life at San Diego State University, "Issues of alleged or perceived favoritism are those which have most commonly presented themselves to me as ethical dilemmas. For example, in offers of on-campus housing in a climate of scarcity, there are those who challenge any preferential treatment whatsoever. As another example, in disciplinary situations in which some participants are extremely vocal or come from influential families or certain ethnic groups, and so on, favoritism has been alleged. For the first example, we have used our associated students' housing advisory board in its capacity to discuss priority questions. The board has endorsed a policy statement. In the second example, the residence hall association council has served as an appeals body when previous dialogue with the staff has not resolved allegations. These two examples make it all sound too ideal to be true, and perhaps that is so; but I believe that our campus leaders model ethical behavior and expect the campus community to do the same. The net result is not always an easily resolved conflict, with everyone in agreement, but at least it is a campus where an ethical climate is a value and often a focus of attention." Hoctor highlights the importance of allowing the campus community to engage in dialogue about the issues and reach an understanding, if not total agreement.

For some leaders surveyed for this study, the issues go beyond favoritism and represent violations of personal integrity. John Bannister, director of financial aid at the University of South Carolina, says, "There have been several times when I have been asked to violate my personal integrity to accommodate an influential individual. These cases involved awarding a scholarship to a relative of a donor who wanted to benefit from the tax laws but at the same time specify the scholarship recipient. To have accepted a donation and let the donor name the recipient would clearly be a violation of the law, as well as unethical. I have always stood firm that to enter into such a scholarship agreement would be against my personal ethics, as well as a violation of the tax law, and I have refused to be a party to any such arrangement."

Favoritism can take on a different aura, as the following situation illustrates. David Butler of the University of Delaware discusses one of the most vexing issues of the housing professional: tripling of students. He recalls, "Department policy stated that freshman students are assigned to residence halls in the order in which space applications are received. For several years, overcrowding had forced the use of triple rooms.

"Black students' space requests are often among the last received, because of continued institutional recruiting efforts beyond the normal deadline for admission to the university. This means that, by policy, a large percentage of our black students would be placed in triple rooms.

"The experience in the early years of overcrowding showed that whenever a black student was in a triple room, he or she was the student who eventually moved. By policy, the three students make that decision. Black students usually did not report being forced to move but rather indicated that it 'just worked out that way.' The psychological atmosphere created by this situation led to a dilemma: Should any special action be taken to change this situation?

"The dilemma was resolved by acting, whenever possible, to avoid assigning black students to triple rooms. This was justifiable in part by the institution's commitment to retention." Butler presents an intriguing perspective on favoritism and puts a positive slant on issues that often represent a negative element for leaders.

For many student services administrators, confronting the issue of "favors" seems unavoidable. Kitchener (1985) notes that this will always be true when demand exceeds resources and when the needs of one individual or group are met at the expense of others. Effective leaders understand their own values and positions on this issue, and they are clear about communicating them when the situation warrants.

Resources

Inadequate funding and the struggle for resources present the greatest challenges to some leaders surveyed for this study. James Archer, Jr., director of the counseling center at the University of Florida, says, "The most difficult challenge for me, as director of a counseling center at a large, research-oriented university, has been the constant struggle for resources. I believe that this struggle is more difficult at a research university because there is more emphasis on graduate education and research. The concept of student development, and the notion that counseling and student services activities are integral to the mission of the university, certainly do not represent widely held values."

John Shingleton, director emeritus of placement services at Michigan State University, agrees that some student services are at a disadvantage in the resource-allocation process: "Adequate budget to properly administer all of the services that should be made available to students at a major university in the area of placement requires tremendous resources and is the greatest obstacle to overcome. Most universities do not recognize how important these services can be to the students and woefully fund them."

Some leaders recognize that their own struggles relate to the institution's. John Corazzini, director of university counseling services at Virginia Commonwealth University, says, "Clearly, the most difficult area of frustration is that of budget. The university suffers from inadequate funding and, ipso facto, so do the counseling services, which I administer. Without adequate funding, it's impossible to expand the staff, meet the staff's needs for equipment, and maintain the decor of the office."

This is particularly true at institutions that are undergoing budget reductions. Thomas Goodale, vice-president for student affairs at Virginia Polytechnic Institute and State University, recalls, "The most difficult challenge I faced as vice-chancellor for student affairs at the University of Denver was maintaining some stability in the face of massive retrenchment. Shortly after I arrived, the board of trustees dismissed the chancellor who had hired me, and the institution found itself with an $8 million operating deficit. With the problem of undercapitalization ($22 million endowment against an $80 million budget), we were faced with layoffs of faculty and staff. We terminated 90 tenured faculty members and dismissed 210 staff members. Of the latter, 40 were in student affairs. My challenge was to try to have some semblance of a student affairs program in the face of a 40 percent loss in market share of student enrollment and erosion of students' confidence in the institution."

Leaders draw on their creativity in coping with such reductions, and Goodale relates his approach: "I played musical chairs, closing the Dean of Students' Office and replacing it with an academic support services component. This was a make-do effort from the remnants of what had been. I tried to preserve program positions in the student center, which had been completed a year previously at a cost of $10.5 million."

Richard Rapp, associate vice-president for student affairs at Boise State University, shares some approaches he has used: "I have used student assistants and volunteers, generated income for my department through publications and fees, and continually promoted the need for additional staffing as ways to deal with this problem."

In a similar situation, Frank Julian, associate professor of legal studies and former vice-president for student development at Murray State University, experienced six budget cuts in seven years. He observes, "Out of these hard times have come some creative solutions to our problems. For instance, we have completely changed our financial management theory, and now each vice-president has total flexibility to spend his portion of the budget as he sees fit to meet his goals. Money can be moved as needed from one office to another, from one line to another, as well as from personnel to operating, from equipment to student wages, and so on. Funds remaining at the end of the year are automatically carried over by the vice-president into the next year. If a position is vacant, the vice-president can choose to freeze it for a period of time and use these salary-saving dollars for other, nonrecurring expenses. Another cost-saving, efficiency-improving idea is our student maintenance force. We have replaced some full-time staff members (through natural attrition) with student employees. Half of our work orders in our campus residence halls are now responded to by our corps of student maintenance workers. This system speeds response time, saves us money, and creates additional on-campus employment opportunities for our students." The times are forcing institutions to direct more energy to generating creative programs (Smith, 1991).

Another creative approach involves staff members. Laurence Smith, vice-president for university marketing and student affairs at Eastern Michigan University, discusses how important it is to think beyond one's own territory: "Basically, universities are structured along very turf-oriented lines. The more difficult times get, the more difficult people become. It is imperative that we get individuals to see that they do not own the resources but that they are stewards of them, and that, ultimately, the overall health of the institution is most important. The ideal approach includes soliciting everyone's ideas and involving people in finding solutions to the difficulties besetting the institution. There must be a widespread belief that the staff can help in restructuring to bring about the changes necessary for survival. I have found, over the years, that staff members deliver substantial results with fewer resources once they are empowered to help create the solutions to these very difficult problems."

Moses Turner, vice-president for student affairs and services at Michigan State University, also believes in involving the staff. He advises, "Ensure that large segments of the organization understand the nature of the problem and share in the solution." Involving people in decisions is a key to these situations and to many others identified by the leaders surveyed for this study.

While Frank Julian, Laurence Smith, and others discuss the creative changes that institutions can adopt, still others describe approaches that individual units can employ. John Shingleton of Michigan State tells how his role of obtaining resources has evolved in an era of retrenchment: "My responsibility was to continually strive to get the necessary money by demonstrating the needs and showing where university funding was not available to go to other sources. For example, the legislature now appropriates $150,000 a year to our unit for collegiate employment research. The legislature also funds an additional $100,000 a year for our alumni placement program."

Resources will continue to be a problem through the next decade, given the economic recession, federal budgetary constraints, and the financial positions of individual institutions (Hauptman, 1991). Some leaders locate their greatest struggles with the priority of student services in the budgeting process; others focus on what budget reductions have meant to their units and to their institutions. Effective approaches to this challenge employ teamwork and creativity.

Managing Time and Multiple Demands

Many of the leaders surveyed for this study cite "too little time" as a major frustration and a constant struggle. The frustration comes from the extraordinary number of demands and the urgency of the issues.

Charles Renneison, vice-chancellor for student affairs at the University of Tennessee, Chattanooga, says, "The greatest frustration in student affairs work is that there is never enough time to do the things you want to accomplish." Ronald Klepcyk, dean of student affairs at Elon College, concurs: "The area of greatest frustration is finding time to complete all tasks associated with my position." Robert Young, vice-president and dean of students at Ripon College, refers to these issues as "the age-old time/responsibility problem— more responsibility than can be handled well within the time constraints."

The number and range of demands are major factors in leaders' struggles with this issue. John Bishop, dean of counseling and student development at the University of Delaware, says, "It became apparent to me soon after I assumed my current position that time-management skills were going to be extremely important to my sanity. The demands on my time came from two primary sources: an increased number of individuals who wished to meet with me for a wide variety of reasons, and an increased amount of paperwork." This is characterized by Dodson, Volp, and McAleenan (1986) as the "eternal frustration," with uncompleted paperwork caused by the intense demands for "people time." Herman Kissiah, dean of students at Lafayette College, shares this frustration over control of one's time and aptly describes the types of individuals and the range of issues that characterize these demands: "In a given hour, I may be involved in discussing the recruitment of student athletes with our director of admissions and our director of financial aid and with the coach, who believes that 'this kid can turn our program around'; listening to why we must have Ping Chong and the Fiji Company appear in our theater next year; explaining to an assistant dean why a particular student organization's plan to spend money really isn't all that good; and trying to explain to an architect why we do not want pink-and-black tile in the bathrooms of our new college center."

Time-related demands sometimes distract leaders from priority issues. Linda Mahan, vice-president for student affairs at the University of Montevallo, discusses her frustration with "the immediacy of daily demands. It often seems that every task is urgent and of equal importance. Under such a barrage of demands, it is easy to be lured to the small, inconsequential, easily managed tasks, which hold the promise of quick completion with minimal effort. These lures, however, are truly full of sound and fury, signifying nothing." Striving to avoid this, Mahan says, "I am learning the satisfaction of time spent determining true priorities and creating time to work well on at least one of these daily—at my most productive working time, and without interruption. The sense of achievement thus attained provides energy for all those other 'must' tasks."

Christ Schwelle, director of the student center at Illinois State University, also takes this approach: "I constantly have to prioritize and have to feel confident that the most important things are getting done and acknowledge that some things may never get done."

Marvin Baron, director of services for international students and scholars at the University of California, Berkeley, talks about the urgency of students' needs and their impact on his priorities: "My greatest obstacle has been my difficulty in limiting time spent on relatively unimportant matters to the small allocation of time that they deserve. I will often spend more time on such matters, because of the anxiety written on a client's face, than the situations really deserve, to the detriment of more important policy issues that require more deliberation. I have done my best to mark out time each week to devote to the latter, and not to allow insignificant matters to intrude at those times."

Dudley Woodard, Jr., professor of higher education and former vice-president for student affairs at the University of

Arizona, identifies this phenomenon as the "minutiae-managing syndrome." He says, "I continually stress, with staff members and others, that we need to periodically review our activities to make certain that they have not replaced major goals and objectives. You need to continue to fight the encroaching bureaucracy and to fight the temptation to yield to the bureaucracy-building activities of others."

In addition to setting priorities, these leaders employ multiple approaches in their struggles to manage their time. John Bishop of the University of Delaware discusses his approach to this dilemma: "My first response was simply to attempt to work more hours. Finding the personal cost of that option to be excessive, I then determined that I had to become more efficient in handling the demands on my time. In my judgment, I could not easily reduce my availability to those individuals who wished to meet with me; to do so might negatively influence my ability to be an effective supervisor, leader, and problem solver. Instead, I concluded, it would be necessary for me to become much more efficient with the paperwork I was required to do. I learned, through the assistance of a very able secretary, to dictate memos, use electronic mail, delegate certain writing tasks, and develop an administrative calendar that permits me to anticipate periods of peak demand, in terms of paperwork. Such changes have increased the efficiency with which I am able to handle the work required of me."

Marian Beane, coordinator of services for international students and scholars at the University of North Carolina, Charlotte, reports, "I used to take work home with me; now I choose *not* to do that as a general rule, but rather to work concentratedly while in the office, even if for long hours, and then be free for other interests after work." Effective leaders learn from others and take advantage of systems and technology to assist them.

Leaders find ways to honor what Barr (1987) calls "being faithful to ourselves—our physical selves, our mental selves, and our psychological selves." Richard Artman of Nebraska Wesleyan University shares additional approaches and carefully notes the importance of asserting personal contact: "Some of the ways I have responded to this challenge are as follows. I have developed a rigorous daily-exercise routine, and I stick to it. I try to exercise during my lunch period and have finally learned to protect this as my time. I meet at the beginning of each week with my secretary, to review the week's agenda, identify important projects and tasks, and schedule the calendar according to these priorities. I attend time-management seminars and put into practice what I have learned. Most recently, use of the Franklin Daily Planner system has helped me tremendously in keeping priorities. The most important thing I have learned is that all agenda are not equal and that I must try to be the person in control of my calendar, rather than allowing others to control my time with their agenda."

Ronald Klepcyk of Elon College also offers a short list of approaches that have worked for him. These include "completing a time log to find out just how my time is normally spent, developing a list of things to do before each work day begins, handling paperwork only once, returning all phone calls the same day they are received, and delegating tasks when appropriate."

James Allan, dean for career services of the State University of New York at Geneseo, talks about variety as a way to manage time and avoid burnout: "In order to avoid burnout, I schedule my day so that a variety of tasks will be performed. I never allow myself to provide individual counseling for an entire day. For example, I may see three students in the morning, three in the afternoon, and fill the rest of the time with a group session or administrative functions. Lunchtime is for physical fitness (jogging or swimming), to allow me time to forget other people's problems and get ready for the next group."

Richard Artman, Ronald Klepcyk, and James Allan know themselves well and employ a variety of time-honored techniques. As leaders struggle with demands on their time, some seek and develop ways to integrate their professional lives with their personal lives. David McIntire, vice-chancellor for student affairs at the University of Missouri, Columbia, says, "Time demands require cheating on my family. Returning to campus in the evening for work-related activities removed me from the right quantity and quality of time with my four growing children. My work schedule, my wife's work schedule, and our sharing childrearing and home chores have proven to be very frustrating. Several solutions have been helpful over the years. When my children were infants or very young, I would alternate taking them with me one at a time on trips and to conferences: diapers and pacifiers substituted for dinner and dancing in faraway cities. As they grew older, I would alternate taking a different one to breakfast each morning before school. My teenagers are seventeen, eighteen, and nineteen, and we still take turns going to breakfast." The leaders surveyed for this study acknowledge the juggling that is required for a full professional and personal life.

Effective leaders can find it daunting to balance competing demands. This challenge has also been noted in the literature. For example, Brown and others (1986) identify five areas of competing demands: relationships with people, job characteristics, work responsibilities, time constraints, and self-expectations. The leaders surveyed for this study approach the challenge of time management very deliberately, with an understanding of themselves and of effective time-management techniques.

Reflections on Leaders' Thoughts

Effective leaders freely acknowledge that the day-to-day practice of the student affairs profession poses challenges and struggles. There is a wide range of such challenges, and they entail issues of racial and cultural diversity, favoritism, confidentiality, time management, and budget, among others. Some (such as confidentiality and favoritism) involve very tangible dilemmas whose resolution may be aided by personal values and/or professional guidelines; with others (such as racial and cultural diversity), the guidelines and models seem more elusive.

Whatever their particular challenges or struggles, leaders engage in processes of resolution that have several common elements. They are able to clearly conceptualize dilemmas. They orient themselves toward solutions, rather than toward problems, and they are thoughtful and deliberate in their actions. According to Kouzes and Posner (1987), challenges can enable the development of skills and abilities that leaders did not know they had and can result in extraordinary accomplishments. Effective leaders find opportunities for professional development in day-to-day struggles.

CHAPTER TEN

Building Identity and Credibility of Student Services Leaders

The effective leaders surveyed for this study are confident in their successes, but they also acknowledge that the path to success has not always been smooth. A variety of issues present challenges and struggles. These leaders named identity and credibility as broad issues, as well as political roles, sexism, and racism. As the leaders discuss these struggles, there is an acknowledgment that, through these struggles, they improve their functioning.

Identity

Some struggles concern issues of identity—personal credibility with constituents, and professional credibility with colleagues. Some leaders also grapple with issues of gender and/ or race. As the leaders talk about their struggles, they illustrate the complexity and challenges of effective student services administration.

Credibility

Some leaders feel that their greatest challenges are concerned with credibility. They talk about this in general terms, and they discuss this issue as it concerns credibility on campus for themselves, for their units, and for the student affairs profession.

David Taylor, vice-president for student affairs at Boise State University, says, "The most difficult challenge is not one single incident but an ongoing, day-to-day challenge. That challenge is one of maintaining trust and credibility in working with various campus groups, primarily students. The student population is an ever-changing one, and although trust and credibility have been established with one generation of students, that does not guarantee that it will carry over to the next. Responses to certain situations, policy development, or other campus events may vary with the issue at hand, the type of student leaders for a given year, the particular staff persons involved, a perspective of a president or a board, and a whole host of other factors." Taylor acknowledges the transience of the populations to whom student services administrators must relate, and realizes that each situation varies.

Taylor goes on to describe how he establishes credibility: "One tries to be as consistent as possible, from situation to situation and from year to year. If the same basic approach is followed in dealing with various situations, problems, issues, and so on, then it is likely that the results will be perceived as in the best interests of all concerned. If there is a basic respect for the rights of students (that is, their rights to be heard and to have input into the process), if there is an effort to keep communication open, and if there is an opportunity for all sides of the particular situation to be presented, then usually the outcome will be satisfactory although not necessarily pleasing to all individuals. Through the process, the actions of the chief student affairs officer should be consistent, and then, hopefully, trust and credibility can be maintained." Taylor stresses that a consistent approach projects an image of evenhandedness, which enhances credibility.

Harrison Morson, dean of student services at Mercer County Community College, talks about issues that extend beyond personal credibility and relate more to the credibility of the student affairs unit on campus: "The challenge I find most critical to the survival and positive image of our student affairs unit is substantiating and fostering the credibility of our particular mission among our academic and administrative support services colleagues. The task is eased if the president recognizes and values the role of student services." Dutton (quoted in Appleton, Briggs, and Rhatigan, 1978) notes that credibility is easier to establish when the president recognizes and values the role of student affairs. According to Morson, "Established parity in organizational reporting lines among deans and vice-presidents by the chief executive officer creates immediate role balance. In the absence of such affirmation by the president, student affairs may readily be perceived in a subservient status—a status which leads to nonsupportive attitudes, low budgetary priority, and a host of related indices, which tend to erode many well-intended programs of student development."

"Working with different presidents when they come on board" has been a challenge for Arthur Sandeen, vice-president for student affairs at the University of Florida. He says, "It is mandatory that the chief student affairs officer understand the new president, convince that person that the student affairs program is important, educate the new president about the goals and objectives of the division, and, most important, obtain the president's support. I have tried to do this primarily by a great deal of personal contact and by doing things that will convince the president that the division and our staff are worthy of that support." Morson and Sandeen both emphasize the importance of presidential support and organizational structure in establishing credibility for student affairs units. This kind of support acknowledges the contributions of student affairs to the achievement of the institution's mission (Barr and Albright, 1990).

Some leaders surveyed for this study feel that the challenge to credibility goes beyond organizational structures and

involves misunderstanding of the student personnel mission
and philosophy. Thomas Flynn, vice-president for student
affairs at Monroe Community College, says, "The lack of
understanding of the philosophy and responsibilities of the
student affairs professional on the community college campus
has been the greatest obstacle. While I encountered this as an
obstacle in the four-year university setting as well, I believe
the very nature of the community college causes greater problems. The student affairs division at Monroe Community College has become very successful in the past few years and is
seen as a resource for the faculty, as well as for students. In
fact, one of the key changes we made is to demonstrate to the
teaching faculty that we are the greatest resource they have.
We are not just student advocates; we are advocates for education, and we provide the necessary link between the student
and the classroom teacher, to foster learning. From a previous
status of almost noninvolvement in academic governance and
other faculty matters, the student affairs division staff has
become significantly immersed in all operations of the college." Flynn notes the importance of educating faculty and
staff members about the assistance and support that student
affairs can provide by establishing student affairs as a vital
campus resource.

Edward Webb, vice-president for student affairs at
Humboldt State University, feels that effective leaders need to
be vigilant and assertive in affirming the essential role of
student services: "My most difficult challenge is the ongoing
one of selling the philosophy and importance of student
affairs to the faculty and to academic administrators. What I
do about it is never-ending. It amounts to educating others
about the role of student affairs in providing a more complete
education for students outside the classroom." Webb cautions
against dichotomizing the roles of faculty members and student affairs staff: "I avoid that dichotomy by stressing the
shared role of all in providing the educational experience.
Faculty members must be involved in out-of-classroom activities, and student affairs must have a place in the classroom.
Most faculty members enjoy their involvement, and so it sells

itself, but they must be recognized and rewarded." Barr and Upcraft (1990) say that this is more likely when faculty members understand the influence of out-of-classroom activities on academic achievement and retention.

Even when student affairs as a whole has credibility on campus, the role of the individual service unit is not necessarily secure. Alan Boyd, director of international student and faculty services at Ohio University, sees a specific identity challenge faced by student service leaders in units that serve specific subgroups on campus: "The most difficult challenge I have faced is dealing with the peripheral nature of international services on the campus. Foreign students are peripheral by definition, and those of us who work with them are therefore on the fringe of the university. Student services are traditionally outside the mainstream, which is by rights academic, and being foreign only exacerbates the problem. I have dealt with it first of all by recognizing it and accepting my position and then by taking initiatives, rather than by waiting for the recognition that I used to feel was rightly ours." The leaders surveyed for this study understand that it is incumbent upon them to help establish the credibility of their specific service units.

Paul Barberini, director of student financial assistance at Arizona State University, offers another example of the challenge of establishing credibility for a single unit: "The greatest obstacle to being successful in my position has been the lack of understanding of the functions of my particular office. Very much like other offices in student affairs, financial assistance is made up of many different programs, with complex rules and a very complex process for students to apply and be awarded funds. This is further complicated by the constant change of federal requirements. It is because of this complexity and constant change that many others throughout the university campus do not have an understanding of either the programs or the process. The only effective means to deal with this obstacle is to find avenues to provide both written and verbal descriptions of program and process. Essentially, it is taking every opportunity to describe the issues regarding

student financial assistance. This becomes somewhat labori-
ous and boring for other staff members throughout the campus; therefore, whenever possible, one issue in financial
assistance should be related to other issues that people are
more concerned with. For example, student loan indebtedness
can easily be related to concerns in career services or to concerns in recruitment and admissions. In other words, it is
possible to hold people's attention if one can find the topic
they are most concerned about and relate the topic in student
financial assistance to that concern, as well as finding some
integrated approach to dealing with concern about both
topics."

Some leaders struggle with issues of credibility that are
quite personal. Robert Nielsen, chief of police at the University of Maryland, Baltimore County, shares his personal slant
on credibility: "The most difficult challenge I ever faced was
gaining acceptance. I went directly from assistant dean of
students to assistant director of public safety. Having never
been a street cop who walked a beat, I had some serious concerns about how the department's fifty or so officers would
respond to my appointment. We had often stood side by side
when the bricks were flying during campus disorders, but
there had to be questions in the minds of some of the officers.
Certainly, my M.A. in English wasn't a particularly impres-
sive credential for the position. The first thing I did was
arrange to attend the police academy, although it was not
required that I do so. The best thing I did was graduate first
in my academy class and be selected by my classmates as a
graduation speaker. It was one way of showing everyone that
I was not afraid to try and that I was as capable as they were.
Training has never stopped since then. Nine years later, I was
selected to attend the National FBI Academy, one of the highest honors a law enforcement administrator can achieve."
Nielsen established his personal credibility by securing credentials that would be credible to his constituents.

Leaders offer wonderful insights into establishing personal credibility. James Quann, registrar and director of student information systems at the University of California,

Santa Cruz, says, "Professional status is something that must be earned. Simply because someone becomes a registrar, dean of students, or whatever, does not in and of itself make one a professional. We must work hard, study hard, learn to become professional, and then always be consistent in acting as a professional ought to act. It helps to teach from time to time. If it is not possible to identify with the faculty, one can always offer noncredit courses designed for staff and student development. Appropriate research activities also pay off in helping us become more professional and earning us recognition as professional partners in the educational enterprise."

Paul Moore, vice-president for student affairs at California State University, Chico, also offers down-to-earth advice about credibility: "Don't worry about it." He does share Quann's belief in self-improvement, however, and he advises, "Worry about developing an ever-widening set of skills and understandings. Be very competent at what you do, and be a scholar. Be committed to quality experiences for students, high performance for yourself, and the central purposes of the institution. If one does these things, recognition will follow. We aren't second-class, we are different, just as development and business officers are different." Moore does not dismiss the importance of credibility, but he says that worrying about it will not establish it. He believes that credibility results from demonstrated competence and scholarly practice.

Political Roles

Another challenge named by the leaders is the necessity of assuming political roles and some leaders' discomfort with their roles. There are indications that student affairs administrators are not adept at utilizing political processes (Barr, Upcraft, and Associates, 1990). It makes sense that a number of the leaders surveyed for this study named politics as one of their most difficult struggles.

William Turner, director of admissions and scholarships at Michigan State University, says the aspect of his job that he least enjoys is "the political game that needs to be

played in order to influence institutional direction." Arthur
Sandeen of the University of Florida sees his political role as
extending beyond his own division: "By far the least enjoya-
ble aspect of the work is political and fundraising activities,
almost always associated with matters outside the division of
student affairs."

Thomas Goodale, vice-president for student affairs at
Virginia Polytechnic Institute and State University, also
acknowledges the importance of politics external to student
affairs. At a previous institution involved in catastrophic budget reductions, he realized very directly the importance of
politics in decision making. He notes how much he learned
from one particular incident: "I failed to get close to the
'consumer' on a number of occasions and found that I was
spending more time with a minority of students, while the
greater good was being left alone. In a time of paucity of
resources, I should have been spending more time with the
decision makers and protecting the turf which everyone was
grabbing, since that was a mode of survival. The lesson I
learned is that higher education has a political basis, which
is pervasive and often diffuse. The chief student affairs officer,
like his or her business and academic counterparts, needs to
spend time in the system."

Samuel Sadler, vice-president for student affairs at the
College of William and Mary, describes the political role very
clearly. He says that he dislikes "the politics which accom-
panies the chief student affairs officer's role. Jockeying for
position, strategizing, coalition building, and lobbying are as
prevalent in higher education as in any political or governmental body I know, and I have always regarded these activities as distractions from my real tasks. But they are present
and must be confronted realistically if a chief student affairs
officer is to serve well the students and staff of his or her
institution." Sadler accepts the fact that some roles that seem
political are essential to success.

Dennis Roberts, dean of student affairs at Lynchburg
College, enlarges this description and highlights some of the
more negative aspects of manipulative political behavior:

"Unquestionably, the presence and prevalence of manipulative political behavior in higher education is my greatest source of frustration. There is one kind of politics, which is simply astute observation and insightful response to what is seen. The other kind of politics is the deliberate manipulation, distortion, or circumvention of people and processes in order to advance one's own agenda. I find this latter type of politics deceitful and destructive; politics of this nature encourages others to behave accordingly, and the community suffers as a result. What is difficult about people who like and use the political game is that some, in fact, seem to be unaware that they are behaving this way and that others around them do not like interacting with this kind of negative overtone. The game seemingly becomes the object of attention for these individuals, rather than the accomplishment of our purposes as educators.

"I have struggled mightily with how to respond to the game of politics. I have been told by some that this is only a natural process and an expected part of human behavior. Ultimately, I cannot accept that manipulation and deceit are eternally a part of our lives. Although this type of politics is difficult to reverse, I can only maintain human hope if I set for myself the goal of undoing this kind of behavior. It is easy to attempt to defeat such political maneuvering through means which only reinforce the political game. The only way I have found of breaking the cycle is to be brutally honest and forthright. This kind of brutality, however, is based on caring for one's colleagues and acquaintances enough to work to reverse self-defeating interpersonal styles which make life miserable for all."

Roberts has found an approach that is comfortable for him, and he takes a constructive approach. Jane Kaspereen, director of the Wellness Center at Chapman College, also sees the need to find a constructive approach, but she chooses a different style: "In order to be successful in student health, we must rise above politics. We must be an island of neutrality."

Whether they choose to be neutral or confrontational, effective leaders clearly recognize the existence of politics, and they establish a style of operating in political environments. Barr, Upcraft, and Associates (1990) also emphasize that political skills can help student affairs practitioners influence campus decision making.

Sexism

Recent reports examining the status of women on college campuses conclude that female faculty and staff members face a hostile work environment, which still includes widespread sex discrimination and sexual harassment (Blum, 1991). Some women leaders surveyed for this study agree that sexism is a cause of struggle.

Discussing the question of her most compelling struggles, Lorrie Rabin, director of counseling and student development at Carnegie-Mellon University, names being female in a largely male organization. Sarah Light, vice-president emeritus for student affairs at Westfield State College, relates that it can be "difficult and lonely when one is not part of the 'good old boys' club." Schlossberg (1989) characterizes this issue as "mattering" and relates it to whether a person is central or marginal. The implications of gender differences go beyond inclusion and exclusion, however. Beverly Prosser Gelwick, former director of the counseling service at Bowdoin College, offers definitive views: "After many years of administration, it is finally becoming clear to me that there are different behavioral and outcome expectations for male and female administrators, from supervisors [and from] professional and support staff. Differences are compounded by the sex of the 'expecting person.' Behaviors expected, tolerated, and/or demanded from male administrators are seen as not appropriate for female administrators. For example, male administrators are expected to administer in a hierarchical manner and are admired when they are strong and authoritarian. Female administrators are expected to be far more nurturing, more egalitarian, and forgiving."

Carmen Jordan-Cox, vice-president for student development at the University of San Francisco, echoes that point:

"It has been my experience that subordinate staff tend to have somewhat unrealistic or skewed expectations of female bosses. Females are expected to be much more relationship oriented and motherly than male counterparts, and it is felt that nurturing of staff should be the dominant trait." This is particularly unfortunate because women who have broken the "glass ceiling" in medium-size nontraditional organizations have demonstrated that effective leaders do not come from just one mold (Rosener, 1990).

Another type of stereotype affects women in the profession: that of the "superwoman." As Carmen Jordan-Cox says, "A female chief who is able to successfully manage a demanding senior position and equally demanding family responsibilities is dubiously labeled a 'superwoman,' who must be sacrificing something important in her personal life or who is on a collision course with reality—she'll burn out soon." Discussing how she handles such biases and inequity in expectations, Jordan-Cox says, "My approach is to be true to myself. I always follow my natural inclinations and the professional style which I believe is best. As a consequence, I have been very successful, getting promotions quickly and accomplishing goals. My sense is that, as more females reach senior management positions, some of the built-in biases will begin to dissipate."

Francine Madrey, vice-president for student affairs at Johnson C. Smith University, would agree: "The fact that two of the other vice-presidents are female makes the job easier and more congenial, usually. Contrary to the notion that women have difficulty working together because they are moody and bitchy, our relationship is much more cooperative. This does not suggest, however, that we have not had our differences (and battles). I think that, as women, we all bring a certain level of sensitivity to the situation. Again, however, the size and the mission of our institution require a high level of sensitivity on the part of the entire executive cabinet." Touching on a related stereotype, Madrey adds, "It is often rumored that black women who have been placed in top-level positions have little interest in mentoring other

women. The 'I have mine, you get yours' attitude is said to
prevail because black women at the top feel threatened by
other aspiring women. I think that on the historically black
college or university campus quite the opposite is true. In my
present situation, there is a strong interest in helping
empower women staff members and students."

Some, like Jordan-Cox and Madrey, believe that things
will improve over time, as more women assume leadership
roles. Others do not believe that improvement will come automatically. Sarah Light of Westfield State says, "Overcoming
such bias does not come without effort, which sometimes
means spending more hours preparing for meetings in which
a female is more apt to be challenged. One must do appropriate homework and soft-sell."

Beyond being prepared, Lorrie Rabin of Carnegie-Mellon relates that what she has done "is to reach out and
develop many relationships with professional people on campus with whom I can share work-related successes and concerns, learn from others, and attempt to accomplish goals."
She goes on to say that she is "eager to join a newly forming
task force on campus, composed of upper-level female managers. This will provide a more structured format for educating myself and networking." As Carmen Jordan-Cox aptly
says, "We need to do more in our various professional training programs to sensitize aspiring professionals to these
biases, so that they can avoid the labeling traps."

Racism

Harrison Morson of Mercer County Community College poignantly portrays the challenges of being a black chief student
affairs officer at a predominantly white institution: "I have
experienced some disconcerting patterns of allegiance and
expectations of leadership. The five presidents I have served
under have all been white. One introduced me to the student
affairs profession and engineered my promotion as the first
dean for students at that institution. A subsequent president
insisted that my title be changed from dean to vice-president,

to match [the titles of] others who reported directly to his office. Both educators may have sincerely recognized my administrative competence and growth potential. However, my recollection is that much of the infusion of minorities into administrative appointments occurred from the late 1960s through the 1970s. This was a period when many minorities were raising their voices, fists, and anything else that would cause folks to pay attention to the racial injustices that continued to plague our democratic society. One has to believe that there were many token appointments, essentially to get some institutions off the hook. I have concluded that it is virtually impossible for anyone to unequivocally set color aside when such appointments are being considered.

"It became apparent to me, generally in subtle ways, that not many of my colleagues openly welcomed black leadership. Even with constant stroking, the degree of trust was a divisive factor. Some truly expected and accepted less in traditional performance standards because of my ethnicity. Others anticipated, particularly many [black] brothers and sisters, *special treatment*. It has been more difficult to address the latter attitudes. The expectation that I would 'cover their ass'—even if there was indefensible evidence of failure to carry out assignments with reasonable proficiency or demonstrated commitment—was a startling reality." The conflict between expectations and allegiance is obvious.

Melvin Terrell, vice-president for student affairs at Northeastern Illinois University, offers another perspective: "Black administrators must travel along a similar path—the path of success which is marked by errors, detours, and hazardous conditions. But even the most adamant apologists for the status quo would concur that, for the black administrator, the road to success is always uphill, with a grade steep enough to test the endurance of the most efficient high-compression engine. And yet when black administrators join the ranks of the other successful 'drivers,' their unique ordeal as they ascend the ranks is seldom acknowledged. Worse yet, the recollection of their trials and tribulations is summarily dismissed or diminished by unsympathetic colleagues, who utilize the old adage about having to 'pay one's dues.' What is not recognized, however, is that the 'administrators' club,' like any other club, does not charge the same dues to all its members, some of whom pay substantially more for essentially the same benefits."

Morson and Terrell both describe how racism adds to the challenges of identity and effective leadership, challenges that thereby become much more complex in an already complex work environment.

Reflections on Leaders' Thoughts

Some leaders surveyed for this study are struggling with issues of identity and credibility. They have moved well beyond viewing the profession as "stillborn" (Penney, 1969) and have come to recognize themselves as professionals by whatever name (Delworth, Hanson, and Associates, 1980). They still struggle with concerns about personal and professional credibility with students and campus colleagues. They struggle with the necessity of their role in campus politics, and some grapple with the challenges presented by sexism and racism.

Issues of identity and credibility are probably endemic to any profession as young as student affairs. Although the functions assumed by professionals in student affairs have a long history, the profession as a formal entity is less than a century old. Professional struggles around identity issues warrant more attention in training programs, in the student affairs profession, and in higher education. The challenge for this generation may well entail moving beyond identity issues—finding new ways to establish credibility on campus through open communication and effective collaboration and by accepting the political agenda as legitimate and establishing professional norms that affirm individual and cultural differences.

CHAPTER ELEVEN

Service as
an Ethic of Care

The leaders surveyed for this study talk about a wide range of topics. In doing so, they offer important insights, identify creative techniques, and share the values that have contributed to their success.

As the leaders discuss their lives and their work, it is apparent that there are some necessary foundations of exemplary leadership. Primary among them are integrity, commitment, and tenacity. Leaders also possess and develop essential skills, primarily leading and following, which emphasize a collaborative style, effective management, and value-driven effort. Leaders with these attributes and skills thrive in supportive campus environments—ethical environments whose institutional missions resonate with leaders' own, environments where leaders participate fully in the decision-making and budgetary processes.

If we understand the emergence of effective leadership as a developmental process, it makes sense that these leaders find themselves—or place themselves—in positions that have the appropriate blend of challenge and support. Armed with supports—their own attributes and skills, and reinforcing environments—leaders face the challenges, struggles, and crises that are attendant to positions in student services. With the positive resolution of challenges, a leader emerges with a strong core character, one that reflects the qualities important to the successful practice of the student affairs profession. The six qualities that mark this strong character are a sense of perspective, an understanding of fairness and the common good, versatility, a sense of adventure, commitment to community, and a generative spirit.

Sense of Perspective

The leaders surveyed for this study demonstrate a clear sense of perspective about their work. They understand why they chose their profession, they are confident that the profession has an important role in higher education, and they are clear that students—their welfare and their development—are of primary importance.

Their sense of perspective also involves acknowledgment of their own vulnerability. They understand that their effectiveness and success depend on forces beyond themselves. These include faculty members, who must be willing to accept and engage them; other institutional leaders, with whom they must collaborate and share responsibilities; and, most important, students, who present leaders with their greatest challenges and their greatest rewards.

Many of these leaders talk about "maintaining perspective." For them, that means understanding that they play important roles for their institutions and for students and that the real essence of their work lies in the human connections they make, not in the authority they assume. This does not mean that they all employ a single style; there is a great variety of styles and approaches represented in this study. It does seem to mean that effective practice of this profession involves an inherent ability to reach out beyond one's assigned unit or set of responsibilities and make connections with other segments of the higher education community.

Understanding of Fairness and the Common Good

For their institutions and functional areas, leaders represent solid and steady forces on behalf of justice, fairness, and the common good. The nature of student services work calls on practitioners to work with complex problems that involve weighty issues, multiple commitments, and sometimes conflicting values. Playing key roles in resolving such problems, leaders operate from a sense of justice and fair play. They can be depended on to see multiple perspectives, keeping the institution, the individual, and the issue in proper focus.

Leaders approach problems and dilemmas with the strong hope that solutions will not be "either/or" propositions, and they search for solutions that represent the common good. This does not mean that everyone agrees with the outcomes; in fact, disagreement is one reality of effective practice. Leaders need to be relational in orientation but also willing to risk positive regard when the situation requires it. Understanding of fairness and the common good guides leaders who are facing dilemmas.

Versatility

Effective leaders function successfully in middle- and upper-level management positions in their institutions. To do so, they possess a wide array of skills, as well as the ability to quickly shift focus and level in order to meet the demands at hand. This means that effective practitioners have to be versatile.

Leaders are skilled in a variety of ways. They have the skills to lead and manage complex organizations. They are skilled in interpersonal interaction and can rapidly adjust their manner as they work with college presidents, faculty and staff colleagues, parents, alumni, and students. All these groups require leaders to be educators and, at times, confidants, advisers, and arbiters of the rules. Leaders also have the political skills to make their agenda the institution's or to find ways for their agenda to support the institution. Of course, they also have the ability to counsel, program, administer, research, and teach. Their experiences have helped them become astute students of human nature, organizational culture, and higher education.

One essential element of these leaders' performance is their ability to focus their attention quickly and adeptly on issues that run the gamut from trivial to global. Within the span of one day, or even one hour, leaders make such sharp shifts, and they view the necessity of doing so as energizing. This does not mean that they do not acknowledge the personal strain that this sometimes causes them, but they often characterize it as double-edged—causing them to struggle, but also bringing them satisfaction.

Sense of Adventure

Leaders are attracted to the profession by its dynamic and challenging nature. After extended careers, they seem sustained by the same sense of adventure that originally drew them to the profession.

Adventurous practitioners need confidence in their own abilities, particularly their intellectual abilities and interpersonal skills. They rely on intellect to conceptualize their work; they rely on interpersonal skills to build bridges to others and to draw others into their vision.

An outgrowth of the adventurous spirit is the confidence to take risks. The willingness to risk enables leaders to test the limits of their own abilities and helps them enable staff members to reach their potential, too. Throughout this study, leaders describe situations in which they have risked and fallen short of their own and others' expectations. They seem able to keep these failures in perspective and not let them limit their willingness to take risks in the future.

The sense of adventure is what prompts leaders to extend themselves beyond the ordinary, sometimes beyond what is reasonable. Coming to grips with their own limits is a continual struggle, as well as an exciting challenge that tests leaders' ability to live "on the edge" and accomplish their goals despite obstacles.

Commitment to Community

Leaders are committed to community. They manifest this commitment in different ways, but it is a strong trend throughout this study.

Some leaders commit themselves to one college or university and devote the majority of their careers to that institution. That institution becomes their community. Approximately one-third of the leaders surveyed for this study have made this kind of commitment. They have what has become an inherent understanding of their institutions and what will benefit their institutions, and they strive to bring those benefits into everything they accomplish.

Some leaders are primarily committed to their functional areas. They believe so strongly in the importance of their functional areas that they are catalysts for progress in their areas, and thus they contribute to the profession in special ways.

Some leaders cross functional areas and assume positions as directors, deans, or vice-presidents. They bring to their positions unique understanding of how the various units in an institution are related. With their fine and diversified experience, they are repositories of a special kind of knowledge.

Other leaders commit themselves to community by establishing communities within their institutions and within their functional areas. By creating "niches," they build bridges between faculty and staff and create highly successful teams within their units. These small teams draw people into commitments to the larger community.

Still other leaders are committed to the professional communities beyond their campuses. Approximately 20 percent of such leaders surveyed for this study have been presi-

dents of national professional organizations. They have pride
in their profession, and they feel that the network of colleagues beyond their campuses is an important community.

These distinctions are not mutually exclusive, and leaders often see themselves as members of multiple communities.
Nevertheless, these five distinct perspectives do emerge. All
the leaders, however, are oriented toward community accomplishments, rather than toward individual achievements. Whatever their special talents and skills, and whatever the arenas
in which they choose to use them, the practitioners surveyed
for this study are enablers and facilitators of community.

Generative Spirit

As they share their diverse experiences, thoughts, and mus-
ings, all the leaders seem to express a generative spirit, one
characterized by the blending of intellect and emotion, conviction about advocacy, and confidence in their ability to
succeed.

Leaders can analyze and evaluate, but they do so with
compassion. They can solve problems, and they do so with
an emphasis on inclusion. They can build structures and
systems, and they do so through collaboration. They seem to
accomplish tasks with skill and determination, and they do
so not with force but with vision.

At the core of this generative spirit is the natural incli-
nation to be an advocate. Leaders assume responsibility to
speak and act on behalf of those whose voices may otherwise
go unheard. They may be the voices of students in the cabinet
room, the voices of international students when their country
is in crisis, or the voices of students of color when decisions
are made about the creation of new programs and services.
Student services leaders seem to assume this role because of a
moral imperative and because they believe that the future of
our institutions and of society rests on the ability to create
communities in which the dignity of all is affirmed.

As they go about their work, leaders incorporate teaching and mentoring as essential and natural components of

the way they function. They assume responsibility for giving of themselves in ways that help others learn and develop. They are skilled taskmasters, which is easy to see in the tangible outcomes of their efforts, but they also accomplish tasks by means of a process that leaves others fully affirmed and enriched as a result of their involvement.

An Ethic of Care

A sense of perspective, understanding of fairness and the common good, versatility, a sense of adventure, commitment to community, a generative spirit—taken together, these six elements represent the commitment to an ethic of care. Canon and Brown (1985) and Gilligan (1982) have characterized this concern for relationship as a higher order skill—an "ethic of care." Kolb (1988) observes that care is expressed in three ways in advanced professional work: "through caring relationships, through careful work, and through moral leadership" (p. 76). The leaders surveyed for this study embody such care.

Dennis Golden, vice-president for student affairs at the University of Louisville, expresses this notion well: "I believe that care for persons is a nonnegotiable component of effective student affairs leadership. There must be a connection between what we do as leaders and why we do it. One of the distinguishing characteristics of a truly educated person is that person's genuine concern for self and others." James Rhatigan, vice-president for student affairs and dean of students at Wichita State University, agrees that the element of care is essential. He reflects, "I would argue that we should try to be effective administrators, but that achievement will be insufficient to the kind of life we seek for ourselves. Success, as I view it, involves an attitude of caring. It takes concrete form in the daily work we do. How do we choose to spend the limited time we have? The functions that have to do with promoting humanistic values are the functions that are most important to me."

To be a leader operating from an ethic of care is an "absorbing errand" (Clark, 1988). Dennis Golden captures the sense of discovery this entails: "What we discover is that becoming a leader is unlike anything else you do. It is both an interior and an exterior transformation. Essentially, you must become person-centered change agents of charity, compassion, and competency. The business of leadership is both *formidable* and *fragile*. It must be wanted, tried, felt, believed, and eventually owned. It also requires that you intensely and passionately involve your value system, beliefs, mind, heart, spirit, and will."

The beneficiaries of this type of leadership are, of course, our students. Golden expresses this idea beautifully: "When one invests his or her time, talents, and treasures in producing an ethic of care bound by a covenant, that person is ready to produce a special kind of student. For me, that special kind of student is achieved when we recruit, retain, and graduate men and women who think logically, write clearly, speak truthfully, decide ethically, function effectively, and exercise a keenly sensitive social conscience. These men and women would be holistically educated—mind, body, heart, emotions, and spirit. They would be the beneficiaries of an ethic of care and a covenant enabling them to become good persons, good professionals, good citizens, and good leaders." Here, Golden articulates the impact of leaders who operate from an ethic of care.

The leaders surveyed for this study were very generous. They have offered valuable insights and perspectives on how exemplary leaders realize their commitments to our profession. Their work, with the ethic of care so central to it, consistently affirms human dignity, individual differences, and the preeminence of community. Our professional heritage, stated so eloquently in *The Student Personnel Point of View* (American Council on Education, 1937, 1949), proves highly relevant and comes alive through the voices of these leaders— themselves inspired and inspiring.

List of Nominators

Appleton, James: president, University of the Redlands; former chief student affairs officer

Banning, James: professor, Colorado State University; former chief student affairs officer

Beer, Ronald: vice-president, student services; National Association of Student Personnel Administrators (NASPA) Region IV-W

Bloland, Paul: professor, University of Southern California; former chief student affairs officer

Blom, Stephen: American College Health Association

Boynton, Asa: International Association of Campus Law Enforcement Administrators

Bridwell, Margaret: director, Student Health Center, University of Maryland, College Park; American College Health Association

Byrnes, Marie: American College Personnel Association (ACPA) Commission XVI

Canon, Harry: professor, Northern Illinois University; former chief student affairs officer

Caswell, James: NASPA Region III

Claar, Joan: dean of students, DePauw University; NASPA Region
IV-E

Cordner, Patricia: ACPA Commission XV

Creamer, Donald: professor, Virginia Polytechnic Institute and
State University; former chief student affairs officer

Cyphers, Robert: American Association of Collegiate Registrars
and Admissions Officers

Duffy, Kevin: NASPA Region I

Duncan, Marsha: vice-president for student affairs, Lehigh University; NASPA Region II

Ebbers, Larry: NASPA past president

Goldberg, Leonard: vice-president for student affairs, University
of Richmond; NASPA Region II

Goodale, Thomas: vice-president for student affairs, Virginia Polytechnic Institute and State University; NASPA past president;
former vice-chancellor for student affairs, University of Denver

Hallenbeck, Daniel: Association of College and University Housing Officers

Halstead, John: NASPA Region V

Herlong, Barbara: Cooperative Education Association

Honea, Rebecca: Cooperative Education Association

Hughes, Marvalene Styles: ACPA past president

Hunter-Hancock, Susan: NASPA Region VI

Jacoby, Barbara: director, Office of Commuter Affairs, University
of Maryland, College Park; National Clearinghouse for Commuter Programs

Kearney, Patricia: assistant vice-chancellor for student affairs, University of California, Davis; ACPA past president

Komives, Susan Bowling: ACPA past president; professor, University of Maryland, College Park; former chief student affairs
officer

Larkin, William: NASPA Region II

Leach, Bobbie: NASPA past president (deceased)

Likins, Jeanne: president, JML Associates, Columbus, Ohio;
ACPA Commission XVII; former director of student life services,
Ohio State University

McIntire, David: vice-chancellor for student affairs, University of Missouri–Columbia; NASPA Region III; former vice-chancellor for student affairs, Appalachian State University

Mann, Peter: College Placement Council

Martin, Dallas: National Association of Student Financial Aid Administrators

Meabon, David: NASPA Region IV-W

Mestenhauser, Josef: National Association of Foreign Student Affairs

Mitchem, Arnold: National Council of Educational Opportunity Associations

Myers, Thomas: vice-president for student affairs, Eastern Kentucky University; NASPA Region III

Nuss, Elizabeth: executive director, NASPA

Pettit, Dawn: Cooperative Education Association

Prior, Carol: Association of College Unions—International

Quatroche, Thomas: professor, State University of New York at Buffalo; former chief student affairs officer

Reinhard, Herbert: president, Frostburg State University; former chief student affairs officer

Rode, Denise: ACPA Commission II

Rooney, Paula: NASPA Region I

Rueckel, Patricia: National Association for Women in Education

Saddlemire, Gerald: professor, Bowling Green State University; former chief student affairs officer (deceased)

Schroeder, Charles: vice-president for student services, Georgia Institute of Technology; ACPA past president; former vice-president for student affairs, University of Northern Colorado

Shaffer, Robert: professor emeritus, Indiana University; former chief student affairs officer

Slavin, Sharon: NASPA Region VI

Smith, Patrick: president, Nazareth College; former chief student affairs officer

Stamatakos, Louis: professor, Michigan State University; former chief student affairs officer

Stott, William: president, Ripon College; former chief student affairs officer

Terrell, Melvin: vice-president for student affairs, Northeastern Illinois University; NASPA Ethnic Minority Task Force

Travelstad, Will: ACPA Commission XV

Vance, Carmen: Association of College and University Housing Officers

Wallenfeldt, Evert: professor, Kent State University; former chief student affairs officer

Weitz, Sue: NASPA Region V

Welch, Harvey: NASPA Region IV-E

Welty, John: president, Indiana University of Pennsylvania; former chief student affairs officer

Werring, Chuck: ACPA Commission III

White, Christopher: president, Gardner Webb College; former chief student affairs officer

Wiley, Mary O'Leary: ACPA Commission VII

Woolston, Valerie: director of international education services, University of Maryland, College Park; National Association of Foreign Student Affairs

RESOURCE B

Respondents to Survey of Effective Leaders

Adamo, Anthony A.: Dean of Student Life and Development, Adelphi University

Adams, Donald: Vice-President for Enrollment Management and Student Life, Drake University

Allan, James L.: Dean for Career Services, State University of New York at Geneseo

Althen, Gary: Foreign Student Adviser, University of Iowa

Anderson, Carl E.: Vice-President for Student Affairs (Emeritus), Howard University

Anderson, Dorothy M.: Dean of Students, Susquehanna University

Andreas, Rosalind, E.: Vice-President for Student Affairs, University of Vermont; former Dean of Students, University of Arizona

Archer, James, Jr.: Director of Counseling Center, University of Florida

Ardaiolo, Frank P.: Vice-President for Student Life, Winthrop College; former Assistant Vice-President and Dean of Students, University of Connecticut

Arnold, Kitty: Director, Career and Placement Services, University of Notre Dame

Artman, Richard B.: Vice-President for Student Affairs, Nebraska Wesleyan University

Bailey, Robert L.: Registrar, University of California, Berkeley

Bannister, John G.: Director of Financial Aid, University of South Carolina

Barberini, Paul G.: Director, Student Financial Assistance, Arizona State University

Baron, Marvin: Director, Services for International Students and Scholars, University of California, Berkeley

Barr, Margaret J.: Vice-Chancellor for Student Affairs, Texas Christian University

Beane, Marian: Coordinator, Services for International Students and Scholars, University of North Carolina, Charlotte

Bebb, Ernest L.: Director, University Union, University of Utah

Beer, Ronald: Vice-President for Student Services, Oklahoma State University

Bishop, John B.: Dean of Counseling and Student Development, University of Delaware

Blankenship, Edward S.: Executive Vice-President and Director, College Division, American Institute for Foreign Study; former Director, International Programs and Exchanges, California State University, Long Beach

Boatman, Sara A.: Associate Professor and Chair, Department of Communication and Theater Arts, Nebraska Wesleyan University; former Director, Campus Activities and Programs, University of Nebraska, Lincoln

Boyd, Alan W.: Director, International Student and Faculty Services, Ohio University

Brattain, William E.: Assistant Vice-President for Student Services, Western Illinois University

Braye, James C.: Director, Career Planning and Placement Center, University of North Carolina at Wilmington

Bridwell, Margaret: Director, Student Health Center, University of Maryland, College Park

Bromley, Max L.: Associate Director of Public Safety, University of South Florida

Bryan, William A.: Vice-Chancellor for Student Affairs, University of North Carolina, Wilmington

Burda, Kenneth F.: Vice-President for Institutional Advancement, State University of New York at New Paltz; former Vice-Chancellor for Student Affairs

Butler, David G.: Director of Housing and Residence Life, University of Delaware

Butler, William R.: Vice-President for Student Affairs, University of Miami

Campbell, Roger H.: Dean of Admissions, Financial Aid and Enrollment Planning, University of Denver

Carlisle, Wayne: Director, Placement and Career Services, Wichita State University (deceased)

Carver, Thomas W.: Vice-President for Student Affairs and Dean of Students, Berry College

Chambers, Judith M.: Vice-President for Student Life, University of the Pacific

Claar, Joan: Dean of Students, DePauw University

Cook, Sherry: Instructor, Marketing Department, Southwest Missouri State University; former Director of Cooperative Education

Corazzini, John G.: Director, University Counseling Services, Virginia Commonwealth University

Correnti, Richard J.: Vice-President, Student Affairs, Florida International University

Coyne, Thomas E.: former Vice-President for Student Services, Western Michigan University (retired)

DeArmond, Murray: Director, Student Health Service, University of Arizona

Delaney, Jean: Director, Office of International Education, University of Colorado, Boulder

Duncan, Marsha: Vice-President for Student Affairs, Lehigh University

Dutton, Thomas B.: Senior Adviser to the Chancellor; former Vice-Chancellor for Student Affairs, University of California, Davis

Edmonds, William B.: Registrar and Director of Admissions (Emeritus), Gainesville College

Engelgau, Gary: Executive Director of Admissions and Records, Texas A & M University

Epting, Jimmy: President, North Greenville College; former Vice-President for Student Development

Etheridge, Robert: Vice-President for Student Affairs (Emeritus), Miami University

Flynn, Thomas R.: Vice-President for Student Affairs, Monroe Community College

Franco, Raymond D.: Assistant Vice-President for Student Affairs and Director of Residential Services, State University of New York at Cortland

Frederiksen, Charles F.: Director of Residence, Iowa State University

Gallineau, Tim: Vice-President for Student Development, Saint Bonaventure University

Gamsky, Neal R.: Vice-President and Dean of Student Affairs, Illinois State University

Gelwick, Beverly P.: independently practicing psychologist; former Director of Counseling Service, Bowdoin College

Gillespie, Cliff: Dean of Admissions, Records, and Information Systems, Middle Tennessee State University

Gilliard, Walter: Associate Dean of Students, University of Dayton

Goldberg, Leonard: Vice-President for Student Affairs, University of Richmond

Golden, Dennis C.: Vice-President for Student Affairs, University of Louisville

Goodale, Thomas: Vice-President for Student Affairs, Virginia Polytechnic Institute and State University; former Vice-Chancellor for Student Affairs, University of Denver

Greisberger, John: Director, Office of International Students and Scholars, Ohio State University

Grimm, James C.: Director of Housing, University of Florida

Gwinn, Donald G.: University Registrar, Northwestern University

Hansen, David A.: Associate Dean for Student Development, University of Nevada, Reno

Heath, Raymond P.: Vice-President for Student Affairs, La Salle University

Herrington, Marvin L.: Chief of Police, Stanford University

Hoctor, Michael B.: Director of Housing and Residential Life, San Diego State University

Horner, David D.: Director, Office for International Students and Scholars, Michigan State University

Jacoby, Barbara: Director, Office of Commuter Affairs, University of Maryland, College Park

Jass, Ruth: Registrar (Emeritus), Bradley University; former Registrar and Director of Institutional Research

Johnston, J. William: Assistant Vice-President for Student Affairs, Southern Methodist University

Jones, Edward L.: Director of University Housing, Southern Illinois University, Carbondale

Jordan-Cox, Carmen A.: Vice-President for Student Development, University of San Francisco

Julian, Frank H.: Associate Professor of Legal Studies, Murray State University; former Vice-President for Student Development

Kaplan, Joshua: Director, Student Health Service, Bowling Green State University

Kaspereen, Jane: Director, Wellness Center, Chapman College

Kearney, Patricia: Assistant Vice-Chancellor for Student Affairs, University of California, Davis

Keeling, Richard P.: Director, Department of Student Health, University of Virginia

Kissiah, Herman C.: Dean of Students, Lafayette College

Klepcyk, Ronald A.: Dean of Student Affairs, Elon College

Klepper, William M.: Dean of Student Life, Trenton State College

Knauer, Brigida: Dean of Students, Occidental College

Koldus, John J.: Vice-President for Student Services, Texas A & M University

Kratzer, David E.: Director, J. Wayne Reitz Union, University of Florida

Kuk, Linda: Vice-President for Student Affairs, State University of New York, College at Cortland

LaLance, Robert C., Jr.: Vice-President for Student Affairs, Middle Tennessee State University

Lazarus, Freyda C.: Director, Office of Cooperative Education, Montclair State College

Levy, Stanley R.: Vice-Chancellor for Student Affairs, University of Illinois at Urbana–Champaign

Light, Sarah L.: Vice-President for Student Affairs (Emeritus), Westfield State College

Likins, Jeanne: President, JML Associates, Columbus, Ohio; former Director of Student Life Services, Ohio State University

Lujan, Sylvia S.: Associate Dean, College of Arts and Sciences and Director, Learning Assistance Center, University of Texas, Pan American

Lyons, James: Dean of Student Affairs (Emeritus), Stanford University

Mable, Phyllis: Vice-President for Student Affairs, Longwood College

McConkey, Douglas F.: Vice-President for Student Affairs, Ball State University

McCray, John H., Jr.: Vice-President for Student Development, University of Rhode Island

McIntire, David: Vice-Chancellor for Student Affairs, University of Missouri, Columbia; former Vice-Chancellor for Student Affairs, Appalachian State University

Mack, Judith K.: Director, Counseling Center, University of California, Davis

McKinley, Donna L.: Dean of Student Affairs, University of Michigan–Dearborn; formerly Assistant Vice-President for Student Affairs, Colorado State University

Madrey, Francine G.: Vice-President for Student Affairs, Johnson C. Smith University

Magoon, Thomas M.: Director (Emeritus), Counseling Center, and Professor (Emeritus) of Education, University of Maryland, College Park

Mahan, Linda C.: Vice-President for Student Affairs, University of Montevallo

Manicur, Alice R.: Vice-President for Student and Educational Services, Frostburg State University

Matthews, Alfred T.: Vice-Chancellor for Student Life, East Carolina University

May, Deborah Orr: Director, Career Planning and Placement, University of Michigan

Mills, George H.: Dean of Admissions, University of Puget Sound

Minetti, Robert H.: Vice President for Student Affairs, Bentley College

Moneta, Larry: Associate Vice-Provost for University Life, University of Pennsylvania; former Director of Housing Services, University of Massachusetts, Amherst

Moore, Paul L.: Vice-President for Student Affairs, California State University, Chico

Morris, Roger J.: Associate Director of Student Development, University of Oregon

Morson, J. Harrison: Dean of Student Services, Mercer County Community College

Myers, Thomas: Vice-President for Student Affairs, Eastern Kentucky University

Nielsen, Robert C.: Chief of Police, University of Maryland, Baltimore County

Nolan, Charles S.: Dean of Undergraduate Admissions, Babson College; former Director of Undergraduate Admissions, Boston College

Ogle, Chris: Associate Dean of Students and Director of Housing, Ripon College

Oleson, Robert E.: Vice-President for Student Affairs, Heidelberg College

Osteen, James M.: Director, Stamp Student Union, University of Maryland, College Park

Ostroth, D. David: Director, University Unions, Student Activities and Recreation, Virginia Polytechnic Institute and State University

Paige, Richard Michael: Associate Professor of International and Intercultural Education, University of Minnesota; former Associate Director, Office of International Education

Paleen, William P.: Director of Residence Life, Cornell University

Pavela, Gary: Director of Judicial Programs, University of Maryland, College Park

Perigo, Donald J.: University Ombudsman, University of Michigan

Pijan, Dorothy M.: Director, Thwing Center, Case Western Reserve University

Powell, C. Randall: Assistant Dean and Director of Placement, School of Business, Indiana University

Pratt, Paul M.: Dean, Cooperative Education, Northeastern University

Preisinger, George J.: Director, University Center and Campus Activities, University of Maryland, Baltimore County

Quann, C. James: University Registrar and Director of Student Information Systems, University of California, Santa Cruz

Rabin, Lorrie E.: Director, Counseling and Student Development Center, Carnegie-Mellon University

Ragans, Sherrill W.: Associate Vice-President for Student Affairs, Florida State University

Rapp, Richard P.: Associate Vice-President for Student Affairs and Director, Career Planning and Placement, Boise State University

Rauker, James J.: Vice-President for Student Affairs, Worcester State College

Ray, Susie: Director, Cooperative Education, Western Carolina University

Rea, Peter: Assistant Academic Dean, Baldwin-Wallace College; former Director of Career Services

Renneisen, Charles M.: Vice-Chancellor for Student Affairs, University of Tennessee at Chattanooga

Rhatigan, James J.: Vice-President for Student Affairs and Dean of Students, Wichita State University

Roberts, Dennis C.: Dean of Student Affairs, Lynchburg College; former Associate Dean of Student Life/Director of Residence Life and Leadership Programs, Southern Methodist University

Rodgers, William P.: Assistant Director, Financial Aid Services, Southeast Region of American College Testing Program; former Director of Financial Aid, University of South Alabama

Ross, David A.: Associate Dean of Student Affairs, Central Connecticut State University

Rouzer, Rob: Director, Wilson Commons/Student Activities, University of Rochester

Rudy, Joel S.: Dean of Students, Ohio University

Sadler, W. Samuel: Vice-President for Student Affairs, College of William and Mary

Sandeen, C. Arthur: Vice-President for Student Affairs, University of Florida

Scheetz, L. Patrick: Director, Collegiate Employment Research Institute, and Assistant Director of Career Development and Placement Services, Michigan State University

Schroeder, Charles: Vice-President for Student Services, Georgia Institute of Technology; former Vice-President for Student Development, Saint Louis University

Schuh, John H.: Associate Vice-President for Student Affairs, Wichita State University

Schwelle, Christ F.: Director, Bone Student Center/Braden Auditorium, Illinois State University

Scott, Nancy A.: Vice-President for Student Affairs, University of Northern Colorado

Seeloff, Eugene R.: Assistant Dean, Career Planning and Placement, School of Engineering and Applied Science, University of Virginia; former Director of Career Services, Lehigh University

Sharkey, Stuart J.: Vice-President for Student Affairs, University of Delaware

Sheridan, Timothy Philip: Director of Student Judicial Programs, Western Illinois University

Shindell, Winston: Director, Indiana Memorial Union, Indiana University

Shingleton, John D.: Director (Emeritus), Placement Service, Michigan State University

Shutt, Bruce T.: Associate Vice-President for Student Affairs and Registrar, University of Georgia

Singer, Stanley L.: Director, Employee Assistance Program,

California State University, Northridge; former Director, Counseling Center

Sivertson, Debra Benoit: Director, Student Health Services, University of Maryland, Baltimore County

Smith, Laurence N.: Vice-President for University Marketing and Student Affairs, Eastern Michigan University

Stimpson, Richard: Assistant Vice-President for Student Affairs, University of Maryland, College Park

Strumpf, Gerry: Director of Orientation, University of Maryland, College Park

Suddarth, Betty M.: Registrar, Purdue University

Swann, Claire: Director of Admissions, University of Georgia

Taylor, David S.: Vice-President for Student Affairs, Boise State University

Terrell, Melvin: Vice-President for Student Affairs, Northeastern Illinois University

Thielen, Tom: Vice-President for Student Affairs, Iowa State University

Thomas, James E.: Registrar, Colorado State University

Thomas, William L., Jr.: Vice-President for Student Affairs, University of Maryland, College Park

Tisue, Garold: Director, Student Resource Center, San Diego State University

Trow, Jo Anne J.: Vice-President for Student Affairs, Oregon State University

Turner, Moses: Vice-President for Student Affairs and Services, Michigan State University

Turner, William H.: Director, Admissions and Scholarships, Michigan State University

Venerable, Wilbur R.: former Director of Admissions and Records, Illinois State University (retired)

Walbolt, Daniel R.: former Vice-President for Student Affairs, University of South Florida

Waldie, Charles R.: Director of Housing, Rutgers—The State University of New Jersey

Ward, Eugene S.: Special Assistant to the Vice-President of Student Affairs, Southern Methodist University; former Director of Housing and Conference Coordination

Webb, Edward M.: Vice-President, Student Affairs, Humboldt State University

Wehrle, Roger E.: Director, Georgia Tech Student Center and Auxiliary Enterprises, Georgia Institute of Technology

Weisinger, Ron: graduate student in Department of Industrial Relations and Human Resources, Rutgers—The State University of New Jersey; former Assistant Director of Student Life, University of Rhode Island

Weston, William D.: Director of Cooperative Education, North Carolina State University

Wood, Nancy V.: Chair, English Department, University of Texas at Arlington; former Director of Study Skills and Tutorial Services, University of Texas at El Paso

Woodard, Dudley B., Jr.: Professor of Higher Education, University of Arizona; former Vice-President for Student Affairs

Woolston, Valerie: Director of International Education Services, University of Maryland, College Park

Yerian, Jean M.: Director, Career Planning and Placement, Virginia Commonwealth University

Young, Robert H.: Vice-President and Dean of Students, Ripon College

Zick, H. Rolan, M.D.: Consulting Surgeon, University of Colorado, Boulder; former Director, Wardenburg Student Health Service

Zimmerman, Kurt: Director, Placement and Career Services, University of Toledo

RESOURCE C

Interview Questions

1. From your personal experience, what is the single most important personal quality which has contributed to your success?
2. What has been the greatest obstacle to being as successful as possible in your position? What have you done about it?
3. What approaches have you found to be effective in motivating staff?
4. What skills have been particularly helpful to you?
5. What was the greatest risk you've taken in your current position?
6. What have you found to be successful in improving race relations on your campus?
7. What strategies have helped you be included in top-level management decisions?
8. How have you established effective working relationships with the following key individuals or groups?
   —Chief academic officer

—Student government president
—Student affairs staff

9.   How have you established effective working relation-
ships with the following key individuals or groups?
—Supervisor
—Chief budget officer
—Student newspaper editor or staff
—Faculty

10.   What has been the most difficult challenge you've faced
in your position? What did you do about it?

11.   What do you think has been the most important factor
from your supervisor's perspective in whether you are
doing an effective job?

12.   Which of the many and varied roles in your position do
you enjoy the most? The least?

13.   We often learn the most from our failures, from errors
in judgment, questionable decisions, or misplaced priorities. What was your greatest failure and what did you
learn from it?

14.   Staff evaluation and performance review are perennial
tasks which trouble many supervisors. What has worked
with you? What would you advise others to avoid doing?

15.   What is the area of greatest frustration in your position?
What have you done to minimize the frustration?

16.   How have you used theory, whether administrative theory or student development theory, in your day-to-day
roles? What has worked best for you?

17.   What is the most serious ethical issue or dilemma you've
faced in your career and what did you do about it?

18.   What have you found to be effective in helping create
cultural and racial diversity on your campus?

19.   What approaches have you found to be successful in
working with individual students, student leaders, or
student groups?

20.   What particular skills have contributed most to your
success as a leader?

21.   How can student affairs staff develop meaningful relationships with faculty?

22. What approaches have been useful in the current climate of budget reductions and reorganization of services?
23. Are there particular characteristics of your institution that have encouraged or enabled your success?
24. Can you identify a crisis—either with an individual or group or the total institution—and discuss your contribution to its resolution?
25. Increasingly, student affairs staff are working with "external constituents"—parents, alumni, and the press. Do you have any insights to give about working with these groups?
26. What have you found to be effective in helping create a positive climate for cultural and racial diversity on your campus?
27. The issue of "professional identity" is one with which many new professionals struggle. Can you offer advice?
28. Are there values you can identify which are essential to your work?

Profile of
Effective Leaders

Gender

The 210 respondents included 157 men (75 percent) and 53 women (25 percent). The total number of respondents who were chief student affairs officers was 76, with 17 (or 22 percent) women and 59 (or 78 percent) men. Of the 134 director respondents, 36 were women (28 percent) and 94 were men (72 percent).

Race

Sixteen leaders responding to the survey were professionals of color. The African American respondents included 6 directors and 8 chief student affairs officers. One director was Hispanic, and one designated the "other race" category.

Age

The mean age for all respondents was forty-eight, with directors averaging forty-seven and chief student affairs officers forty-nine. Directors had both the youngest respondent (thirty) and the oldest (sixty-eight). No chief student affairs officer was under thirty-five.

Experience

The mean number of years of experience in higher education for all respondents was twenty-two, with chief student affairs officers averaging twenty-four and directors twenty. The mean average years of experience in the current position was eleven for chief student affairs officers, with a range of one to thirty. For directors, the average was nine, with a range of one to thirty-three.

Educational Attainment

The highest degrees for all respondents were as follows: the doctorate, 61 percent; the master's degree, 36 percent; and the baccalaureate degree, 3 percent. Among directors, 48 percent had the doctorate, 47 percent had the master's degree, and 5 percent had the bachelor's degree. Among chief student affairs officers, 83 percent had the doctorate and 17 percent had the master's as the highest degree.

Graduate School Affiliations

Table 1 shows that Michigan State University had the highest number of total graduate degrees (twenty-four), followed by Indiana University (twenty-one) and by Southern Illinois University and the University of Michigan (ten each). The eleven schools listed in Table 1 awarded 44 percent of the doctorates reported by the respondents and 37 percent of the master's degrees.

Professional Associations

Approximately one-third of both groups of respondents had served as presidents of national associations. Among chief student affairs officers, twelve had served as president of the National Association of Student Personnel Administrators, six had served as president of the American College Personnel Association, and one had served as president of the National Association of Women Deans, Administrators, and Counselors. Over one-third of the directors had served as presidents of national associations.

Table 1. Graduate Degree Institutions.

Institution	Number Graduating		
	Master's	Doctorate	Total
Michigan State University	10	14	24
Indiana University	12	9	21
Southern Illinois University	7	3	10
University of Michigan	5	5	10
Ohio State University	3	5	8
Ohio University	4	3	7
University of Iowa	4	2	6
University of Maryland, College Park	2	4	6
University of Pittsburgh	3	2	5
Bowling Green State University	5	0	5
State University of New York, College at Buffalo	2	3	5

REFERENCES

Association of American Colleges. *Integrity in the College Curriculum: A Report to the College Community.* Washington, D.C.: Association of American Colleges, 1985.

American Association of University Professors. *Policy Documents and Reports, 1984 Edition.* Washington, D.C.: American Association of University Professors, 1984.

American College Personnel Association Generativity Project. *Bob Shaffer on the Future of the Student Personnel Profession.* Alexandria, Va.: American College Personnel Association, 1987. Videotape.

American College Personnel Association Generativity Project. *Esther Lloyd-Jones: Perspectives on the Student Personnel Point of View, 1937–1987.* Alexandria, Va.: American College Personnel Association, 1987. Videotape.

American College Personnel Association Generativity Project. *C. Gilbert Wrenn on Student Personnel: Origins, Organizations, and Outlooks.* Alexandria, Va.: American College Personnel Association, 1989. Videotape.

American Council on Education. *The Student Personnel Point of View.* Washington, D.C.: American Council on Education, 1937.

American Council on Education. *The Student Personnel Point of View.* (Rev. ed.) Washington, D.C.: American Council on Education, 1949.

Appleton, J. R., Briggs, C. M., and Rhatigan, J. J. *Pieces of Eight.* Portland, Oreg.: National Association of Student Personnel Administrators, 1978.

Astin, A. W., and Scherrei, R. A. *Maximizing Leadership Effectiveness.* San Francisco: Jossey-Bass, 1980.

Barr, M. J. "Individual and Institutional Integrity." *NASPA Journal,* 1987, *24*(4), 2–5.

Barr, M. J., and Albright, R. L. "Rethinking the Organizational Role of Student Affairs." In M. J. Barr, M. L. Upcraft, and Associates (eds.), *New Futures for Student Affairs.* San Francisco: Jossey-Bass, 1990.

Barr, M. J., Keating, L. A., and Associates. *Developing Effective Student Services Programs: Systematic Approaches for Practitioners.* San Francisco: Jossey-Bass, 1985.

Barr, M. J., Upcraft, M. L., and Associates. *New Futures for Student Affairs.* San Francisco: Jossey-Bass, 1990.

Bass, B. *Stogdill's Handbook of Leadership: A Survey of Theory and Research.* (Rev. ed.) New York: Free Press, 1981.

Bass, B., and Stogdill, R. M. *Bass and Stogdill's Handbook of Leadership: Theory, Research, and Managerial Applications.* (3rd ed.) New York: Free Press, 1990.

Baxter Magolda, M. B., and Magolda, P. M. "Student Activism: A Historical Perspective." In K. M. Miser (ed.), *Student Affairs and Campus Dissent: Reflections of the Past and Challenge for the Future.* Washington, D.C.: National Association of Student Personnel Administrators, 1988.

Bennett, W. J. *Study Group on the State of Learning in the Humanities in Higher Education: To Reclaim a Legacy.* Washington, D.C.: National Endowment for the Humanities, 1985.

Bennis, W. G. *On Becoming a Leader.* Reading, Mass.: Addison-Wesley, 1989a.

Bennis, W. G. *Why Leaders Can't Lead: The Unconscious Conspiracy Continues.* San Francisco: Jossey-Bass, 1989b.

Bennis, W. G., and Nanus, B. *Leaders: The Strategies for Taking Charge.* New York: HarperCollins, 1985.

Bensimon, E., Neuman, A., and Birnbaum, R. *Making Sense of Administrative Leadership: The "L" Word in Higher Education Leadership.* ASHE-ERIC Higher Education Report, no. 1. Washington, D.C.: George Washington University, 1989.

Birnbaum, R. *How Colleges Work: The Cybernetics of Academic Organization and Leadership.* San Francisco: Jossey-Bass, 1988.

Blum, D. E. "Environment Still Hostile to Women in Academe, New Evidence Indicates." *Chronicle of Higher Education,* Oct. 9, 1991, pp. A1, A20.

Blumenstyk, G., and Crystal Cage, M. "Dire State Economies Force Tough Choices on Many Universities." *Chronicle of Higher Education,* June 12, 1991, pp. A1, A12.

Bowen, H. R., and Schuster, J. H. *American Professors: A National Resource Imperiled.* New York: Oxford University Press, 1986.

Boyer, E. L. *College: The Undergraduate Experience in America.* New York: HarperCollins, 1987.

Brown, R. D. *Student Development in Tomorrow's Higher Education: A Return to the Academy.* Washington, D.C.: American College Personnel Association, 1972.

Brown, R. D. "Creating an Ethical Community." In H. J. Canon and R. D. Brown (eds.), *Applied Ethics in Student Services.* New Directions for Student Services, no. 30. San Francisco: Jossey-Bass, 1985.

Brown, R. D. *Performance Appraisal as a Tool for Staff Development.* New Directions for Student Services, no. 43. San Francisco: Jossey-Bass, 1988a.

Brown, R. D. "Editorial." *Journal of College Student Development,* 1988b, *29*(2), 99.

Brown, R. D., and others. "Studying Stress Among Student Services Professionals: An Interactional Approach." *NASPA Journal,* 1986, *23*(4), 2-9.

Brown, S. "Approaches to Collaboration Between Academic and Student Affairs: An Overview." *NASPA Journal,* 1989, *26*(1), 2-7.

Burns, J. M. *Leadership.* New York: HarperCollins, 1978.

Cameron, K. S. "Institutional Effectiveness in Higher Education: An Introduction." *Review of Higher Education,* 1985, *9,* 1-4.

Canon, H. J. "Guiding Standards and Principles." In U. Delworth, G. R. Hanson, and Associates (eds.), *Student Services: A Handbook for the Profession.* (2nd ed.) San Francisco: Jossey-Bass, 1989.

Canon, H. J., and Brown, R. D. "How to Think About Professional Ethics." In H. J. Canon and R. D. Brown (eds.), *Applied Ethics in Student Services.* New Directions for Student Services, no. 30. San Francisco: Jossey-Bass, 1985.

Caple, R. B. "Expanding the Horizon." *Journal of College Student Development,* 1991, *32*(5), 111–133.

Caple, R. B., and Newton, F. B. "Leadership in Student Affairs." In T. K. Miller, R. B. Winston, and Associates (eds.), *Administration and Leadership in Student Affairs.* Muncie, Ind.: Accelerated Development, 1991.

Carnegie Foundation for the Advancement of Teaching. *Campus Life: In Search of Community.* Princeton, N.J.: Princeton University Press, 1990.

Chaffee, E. E., and Tierney, W. C. *Collegiate Culture and Leadership Strategies.* New York: American Council on Education, 1988.

Clark, B. R. "The Absorbing Errand." Paper presented at the American Association of Higher Education's National Conference on Higher Education, Washington, D.C., March 1988.

Clark, D. L. "Emerging Paradigms in Organizational Theory and Research." In Y. S. Lincoln (ed.), *Organizational Theory and Inquiry: The Paradigm Revolution.* Newbury Park, Calif.: Sage, 1985.

Coles, R. *The Call of Stories.* Boston: Houghton Mifflin, 1989.

Council for the Advancement of Standards. *CAS Standards for Student Services/Development Programs.* Iowa City, Iowa: American College Testing Service, 1986.

Creeden, J. E. "Student Affairs Biases as a Barrier to Collaboration: A Point of View." *NASPA Journal,* 1989, *26*(1), 60–63.

Dalton, J. C. "Enhancing Staff Knowledge and Skills." In U. Delworth, G. R. Hanson, and Associates (eds.), *Student Services: A Handbook for the Profession.* (2nd ed.) San Francisco: Jossey-Bass, 1989.

DeCoster, D., and Krager, L. "Student Affairs Professionals and the Student Press." In J. Schuh, *Enhancing Relationships with the Student Press.* New Directions for Student Services, no. 33. San Francisco: Jossey-Bass, 1986.

Deegan, W. L. *Managing Student Affairs Programs: Methods, Models, and Muddles.* Palm Springs, Calif.: ETC Publications, 1981.

Delworth, U., Hanson, G. R., and Associates (eds.). *Student Services: A Handbook for the Profession.* San Francisco: Jossey-Bass, 1980.

Delworth, U., Hanson, G. R., and Associates (eds.). *Student Services: A Handbook for the Profession.* (2nd ed.) San Francisco: Jossey-Bass, 1989.

DePree, M. *Leadership Is an Art.* New York: Doubleday, 1989.

DiBrito, F. G. "Cases of Interpersonal Loyalty Between Chief Student Affairs Officers and Their Superordinate and Subordinates." Unpublished doctoral dissertation, Texas A & M University, 1990.

Dodson, D. P., Volp, P. M., and McAleenan, A. C. "The View from the Top: The Small College Chief Student Affairs Officer's Experience." In G. D. Kuh and A. C. McAleeran (eds.), *Private Dreams, Shared Visions: Student Affairs Work in Small Colleges.* Monograph Series, no. 5. Washington, D.C.: National Association of Student Personnel Administrators, 1986.

Downey, K. M. "Majoring in Self-Interest, Minoring in Apathy: A Challenge for the New Activists." In D. A. DeCoster and P. Mable (eds.), *Understanding Today's Students.* New Directions for Student Services, no. 16. San Francisco: Jossey-Bass, 1981.

Dressel, P. L. *Administrative Leadership: Effective and Responsive Decision Making in Higher Education.* San Francisco: Jossey-Bass, 1981.

Dutton, T., and Rickard, S. T. "Organizing Student Services." In U. Delworth, G. R. Hanson, and Associates (eds.), *Student Services: A Handbook for the Profession.* (2nd ed.) San Francisco: Jossey-Bass, 1989.

Fenske, R. H. "Historical Foundations." In U. Delworth, G. R. Hanson, and Associates (eds.), *Student Services: A Handbook for the Profession.* San Francisco: Jossey-Bass, 1980.

Fenske, R. H. "Evolution of the Student Services Profession." In U. Delworth, G. R. Hanson, and Associates (eds.), *Stu-

dent Services: A Handbook for the Profession. (2nd ed.) San Francisco: Jossey-Bass, 1989.

Fink, R. A. "Vision: An Essential Component of Leadership." *Profile,* 1988, *8,* 1–5.

Fisher, J. L., Tack, M. W., and Wheeler, K. J. *The Effective College President.* New York: American Council on Education, 1988.

Fleming, J. *Blacks in College: A Comparative Study of Students' Success in Black and White Institutions.* San Francisco: Jossey-Bass, 1984.

Gardner, J. W. *On Leadership.* New York: Free Press, 1990.

Garland, P. *Serving More Than Students: A Critical Need for College Student Personnel Services.* ASHE-ERIC Higher Education Report, no. 7. Washington, D.C.: Association for the Study of Higher Education, 1985.

Gilley, J. W. "The Past Is Prologue: A Perspective on Leadership." *Educational Record,* 1985, *66*(3), 24–29.

Gilligan, C. *In a Different Voice.* Cambridge, Mass.: Harvard University Press, 1982.

Green, M. F. *Leaders for a New Era.* New York: American Council on Education, 1988.

Green, M. F. (ed.). *Minorities on Campus.* Washington, D.C.: American Council on Education, 1989.

Hauptman, A. M. "Meeting the Challenge: Doing More with Less in the 1990s." *Educational Record,* 1991, *72*(2), 6–13.

Heller, T., and Van Til, J. "Leadership and Followership: Some Summary Propositions." *Journal of Applied Behavioral Science,* 1982, *18,* 405–414.

Hersey, P., and Blanchard, K. H. *Management of Organizational Behavior.* Englewood Cliffs, N.J.: Prentice-Hall, 1988.

Heyns, R. W. "Leadership Lessons from Watergate." *Educational Record,* 1973, *54,* 172–174.

Hickman, C. R., and Silva, M. A. *Creating Excellence.* Ontario, Canada: New American Library, 1984.

Jacoby, B. "Today's Students: Diverse Needs Require Comprehensive Responses." In T. K. Miller and R. B. Winston (eds.), *Administration and Leadership in Student Affairs.* Muncie, Ind.: Accelerated Development, 1991.

Kauffman, J. F. "The College and University Presidency." In M. W. Peterson and L. A. Mets (eds.), *Key Resources on Higher Education Governance, Management, and Leadership.* San Francisco: Jossey-Bass, 1987.

Kazantzakis, N. *Zorba the Greek.* New York: Ballantine Books, 1964.

Keller, G. *Academic Strategy.* Baltimore: Johns Hopkins University Press, 1983.

Kerr, C. *Presidents Make a Difference: Strengthening Leadership in Colleges and Universities.* Washington, D.C.: Association of Governing Boards of Universities and Colleges, 1984.

Kerr, C., and Gade, M. L. *The Many Lives of Academic Presidents: Time, Place, and Character.* Washington, D.C.: Association of Governing Boards of Universities and Colleges, 1986.

Kitchener, K. S. "Ethical Principles and Ethical Decisions in Student Affairs." In H. J. Canon and R. D. Brown (eds.), *Applied Ethics in Student Services.* New Directions for Student Services, no. 30. San Francisco: Jossey-Bass, 1985.

Knefelkamp, L. L. "A Developmental Perspective on the Student Voice." In D. DeCoster and P. Mable (eds.), *Understanding Today's Students.* New Directions for Student Services, no. 16. San Francisco: Jossey-Bass, 1981.

Knefelkamp, L. L. "Are We on Common Ground?" Keynote address to the national conference of the National Association of Student Personnel Administrators, Denver, March 1989.

Knefelkamp, L. L., Parker, C. A., and Widick, C. "Student Development." In U. Delworth, G. R. Hanson, and Associates (eds.), *Student Services: A Handbook for the Profession.* (2nd ed.) San Francisco: Jossey-Bass, 1989.

Kolb, D. A. "Integrity, Advanced Professional Development, and Learning." In S. Srivastva and Associates (eds.), *Executive Integrity: The Search for High Human Values in Organizational Life.* San Francisco: Jossey-Bass, 1988.

Komives, S. R. "Gender Differences in the Relationship of Hall Directors' Transformational and Transactional Leadership and Achieving Styles." *Journal of College Student Development,* 1991, *32*(2), 155–165.

Koontz, H., and O'Donnell, C. *Principles of Management: An Analysis of Managerial Functions.* New York: McGraw-Hill, 1972.

Kouzes, J. M. "When Leadership Collides with Loyalty." In W. E. Rosenbach and R. L. Taylor (eds.), *Contemporary Issues in Leadership.* Boulder, Colo.: Westview Press, 1989.

Kouzes, J. M., and Posner, B. Z. *The Leadership Challenge: How to Get Extraordinary Things Done in Organizations.* San Francisco: Jossey-Bass, 1987.

Kuh, G. D. "What Is Extraordinary About Student Affairs Organizations?" *NASPA Journal,* 1985, *23*(2), 31–43.

Kuh, G. D., Evans, N. J., and Duke, J. A. "Career Patterns of Chief Student Affairs Officers." *NASPA Journal,* 1983, *21*(1), 39–47.

Kuh, G. D., and Nuss, E. M. "Evaluating Financial Management in Student Affairs." In J. Schuh (ed.), *Financial Management for Student Affairs Administrators.* ACPA Media Publication, no. 48. Alexandria, Va.: American College Personnel Association, 1990.

Kuh, G. D., Schuh, J. H., Whitt, E. J., and Associates (eds.). *Involving Colleges: Successful Approaches to Fostering Student Learning and Development Outside the Classroom.* San Francisco: Jossey-Bass, 1991.

Kuh, G. D., Whitt, E. J., and Shedd, J. D. *Student Affairs Work, 2001: A Paradigmatic Odyssey.* ACPA Media Publication, no. 42. Alexandria, Va.: American College Personnel Association, 1987.

Lawson, J. D. "Student Government Leaders." In D. C. Roberts (ed.), *Student Leadership Programs in Higher Education.* ACPA Media Publication, no. 30. Carbondale, Ill.: American College Personnel Association, 1981.

Leatherman, C. "Colleges' Failure to Tackle Pressing Problems in 1980s Laid to Lack of Collaboration by Professors and Administrators." *Chronicle of Higher Education,* Jan. 23, 1991, pp. A1, A12.

Lincoln, Y. S., and Guba, E. *Naturalistic Inquiry.* Newbury Park, Calif.: Sage, 1985.

Lipman-Blumen, J. *Connective Leadership: Female Leadership Styles Meeting the Challenge.* Unpublished paper, Peter F. Drucker Graduate Management Center, 1989.

Lunsford, L. W. "Chief Student Affairs Officer: The Ladder to the Top." *NASPA Journal,* 1984, *22*(1), 48–56.

Maccoby, M. *The Gamesman: The New Corporate Leaders.* New York: Simon & Schuster, 1976.

Martin, W. B. "Mission: A Statement of Identity and Direction." In J. Green, A. Levine, and Associates (eds.), *Opportunity in Adversity: How Colleges Can Succeed in Hard Times.* San Francisco: Jossey-Bass, 1985.

Massey, W., and Zemsky, R. "The Lattice and the Ratchet." *Policy Perspectives,* 1990, *2*(4), 1–8.

Miller, T. K., and Prince, J. S. *The Future of Student Affairs: A Guide to Student Development for Tomorrow's Higher Education.* San Francisco: Jossey-Bass, 1976.

Miller, T. K., Winston, R. B., and Associates (eds.). *Administration and Leadership in Student Affairs.* Muncie, Ind.: Accelerated Development, 1991.

Miser, K. M. (ed.). *Student Affairs and Campus Dissent: Reflections of the Past and Challenge for the Future.* Washington, D.C.: National Association of Student Personnel Administrators, 1988.

Mueller, K. H. *Student Personnel Work in Higher Education.* Boston: Houghton Mifflin, 1961.

National Association of Student Personnel Administrators. *A Perspective on Student Affairs.* Iowa City, Iowa: American College Testing Service, 1987.

Patton, M. J. "Qualitative Research on College Students: Philosophical and Methodological Comparisons with the Quantitative Approach." *Journal of College Student Development,* 1991, *32*(5), 389–396.

Penney, J. F. "College Student Personnel: A Profession Stillborn." *Personnel and Guidance Journal,* 1969, *47,* 958–962.

Peters, T., and Austin, N. *A Passion for Excellence: The Leadership Difference.* New York: Random House, 1985.

Peters, T., and Waterman, R., Jr. *In Search of Excellence: Les-*

sons from America's Best-Run Companies. New York: HarperCollins, 1982.

Peterson, M. W., and Mets, L. A. *Key Resources on Higher
Education Governance, Management, and Leadership.* San
Francisco: Jossey-Bass, 1987.

Priest, D., Alphenaar, W. J., and Boer, W. J. "Long-Range
Planning: Implications and Applications for the Chief Student Personnel Administrator." *NASPA Journal,* 1980, *18,*
2-7.

Reger, M. P., and Hyman, R. E. "Academic and Student
Affairs: Perceptions on Partnerships." *NASPA Journal,*
1989, *26*(1), 64-70.

Rickard, S. T. "The Role of the Chief Student Personnel
Administrator Revisited." *NASPA Journal,* 1972, *9*(3),
219-226.

Rickard, S. T. "Staff Selection in Student Affairs: Common
Problems and Their Prevention." *NASPA Journal,* 1984, *22,*
17-25.

Rickard, S. T. "Career Pathways of Chief Student Affairs Officers: Making Room at the Top for Females and Minorities." *NASPA Journal,* 1985, *22*(4), 52-60.

Rosener, J. B. "Ways Women Lead." *Harvard Business
Review,* 1990, *68,* 119-125.

Rudolph, F. *The American College and University: A History.*
New York: Knopf, 1962.

Saddlemire, G. L., and Rentz, A. L. *Student Affairs: A Profession's Heritage.* ACPA Media Publication, no. 40. Alexandria, Va.: American College Personnel Association, 1986.

Sagaria, M. A. "Administrative Mobility and Gender: Patterns
and Processes in Higher Education." *Journal of Higher
Education,* 1988, *59,* 305-326.

Sandeen, A. "Issues Influencing the Organization of Student
Affairs." In U. Delworth, G. R. Hanson, and Associates
(eds.), *Student Services: A Handbook for the Profession.* (2nd
ed.) San Francisco: Jossey-Bass, 1989.

Sandeen, A. *The Chief Student Affairs Officer: Leader, Manager, Mediator, Educator.* San Francisco: Jossey-Bass, 1991.

Sanford, N. *Self and Society.* New York: Atherton Press, 1966.

Schlossberg, N. K. "Marginality and Mattering: Key Issues in Building Community." In D. C. Roberts (ed.), *Designing Campus Activities to Foster a Sense of Community.* New Directions for Student Services, no. 48. San Francisco: Jossey-Bass, 1989.

Schön, D. A. *Educating the Reflective Practitioner: A New Design for Teaching and Learning in the Professions.* San Francisco: Jossey-Bass, 1987.

Schuh, J. H. (ed.). *Enhancing Relationships with the Student Press.* New Directions for Student Services, no. 33. San Francisco: Jossey-Bass, 1986.

Schuh, J., and Carlisle, W. "Supervision and Evaluation: Selected Topics for Emerging Professionals." In T. K. Miller and R. B. Winston (eds.), *Administration and Leadership in Student Affairs.* Muncie, Ind.: Accelerated Development, 1991.

Shaffer, R. H. "Student Affairs: Retrospect and Prospect." Paper presented at joint conference of the American College Personnel Association and the National Association of Student Personnel Administrators, Chicago, March 1987.

Siegel, D. "Crisis Management: The Campus Responds." *Educational Record,* 1991, 72, 14–19.

Simmel, G. *The Sociology of Georg Simmel.* (Kurt Wolff, ed. and trans.) New York: Free Press, 1950.

Smith, D. G. *The Challenge of Diversity: Involvement or Alienation in the Academy?* ASHE-ERIC Higher Education Report, no. 5. Washington, D.C.: Association for the Study of Higher Education, 1989.

Smith, P. "Beyond Budgets: Changing for the Better." *Educational Record,* 1991, 72(2), 26–29.

Srivastva, S., and Associates (eds.). *Executive Integrity: The Search for High Human Values in Organizational Life.* San Francisco: Jossey-Bass, 1988.

Stogdill, R. M. "Personal Factors Associated with Leadership: A Survey of the Literature." *Journal of Psychology,* 1948, 25, 35–71.

Tichy, N. M., and Devanna, M. *The Transformational Leader.* New York: Wiley, 1986.

Thrash, P. "The Changing Role of the Student Personnel Dean." *Journal of the National Association of Women Deans and Counselors*, 1965, *29*, 10–13.

Tripp, P. A. "The Dean: Leader, Teacher, and Learner." Paper presented at the annual meeting of the National Association of Student Personnel Administrators, Boston, April 1970a.

Tripp, P. A. "The Role of the Dean of Students in the Academic Community: Servant or Leader?" Paper presented at the annual meeting of the National Association of Student Personnel Administrators, Boston, April 1970b.

Upcraft, M. L., and Barr, M. J. *Managing Student Affairs Effectively.* New Directions for Student Services, no. 41. San Francisco: Jossey-Bass, 1988.

Whetten, D. A., and Cameron, K. S. "Administrative Effectiveness in Higher Education." *Review of Higher Education*, 1985, *9*, 35–49.

Whitt, E. J. "Artful Science: A Primer on Qualitative Research Methods." *Journal of College Student Development*, 1991, *32*(5), 406–415.

Winston, R. B. "Counseling and Advising." In U. Delworth, G. R. Hanson, and Associates (eds.), *Student Services: A Handbook for the Profession.* (2nd ed.) San Francisco: Jossey-Bass, 1989.

Wolfe, T. *The Right Stuff.* New York: Bantam Books, 1980.

Yarris, E. "Counseling." In A. L. Rentz and G. L. Saddlemire (eds.), *Student Affairs Functions in Higher Education.* Springfield, Ill.: Thomas, 1988.

Young, R. "Education in the Essential Values of Student Affairs Work." *Journal of College Student Development*, 1991, *32*(2), 109–115.

Yukl, G. *Leadership in Organizations.* Englewood Cliffs, N.J.: Prentice-Hall, 1981.

Yukl, G. *Leadership in Organizations.* (2nd ed.) Englewood Cliffs, N.J.: Prentice-Hall, 1989.

Name Index

Subject Index

A

Action, and leading, 56–60
Adventure, sense of, 200–201
AIDS, 27–28
American Association of University Professors, 7
American College Health Association (ACHA), Task Force on AIDS of, 27–28
American College Personnel Association, 4; Generativity Project, 5–6
American Council on Education, 4, 61, 204
Association of American Colleges, 7
Attitude: "can do," 33, 73–74; positive, 29–33

B

Budget, scarcity in, 174–175
Budgeting process, involvement in, 77–80

C

Care, ethic of, 203–204
Carnegie Foundation for the Advancement of Teaching, 8, 43
Collaborative style, 41–43, 61–62
Commitment, 18, 29; to community, 201–202; enthusiasm and joy as, 30–33; passion as, 33–34; positive attitude as, 29–30
Common good, understanding of, 199

Communication, 47–51
Community, commitment to, 201–202
Confidentiality, 168–170
Council of Student Personnel Associations in Higher Education, Commission on Professional Development of, 4–5
Courage, 24–26
Credibility, of leaders, 184–189
Crises; campus protests as, 151–155; environmental conditions as, 147–151; individual student, 161–163; international conflicts as, 156–158; leadership role in, 145–147; politics and expectations as, 158–161
Culture: institutional, 43–44; of leadership, 2

D

Decision making, institutional, 72–77
Diversity: coping with, 165–168; and leadership, 53–54; and understanding of students, 86–87

E

Editors, of student newspapers, 100–104
Emergent paradigm, 10
Enthusiasm, 30–33
Environment: constructive, 54–55; crises in, 147–151; supportive, 63, 80–81. See also Institutions

246